MW01378627

GARDEN STYLES

WRITER: KATHLEEN S. DICKASON

CONSULTANT: C. COLSTON BURRELL

PUBLICATIONS INTERNATIONAL, LTD.

Louis Weber, C.E.O.
Publications International, Ltd.
7373 North Cicero Avenue
Lincolnwood, Illinois 60646

8 7 6 5 4 3 2 1

ISBN: 0-7853-1685-X
Library of Congress Catalog Card Number: 95-72543

Kathleen S. Dickason is an active gardener and horticultural writer whose specialties are garden history and design. Her articles have appeared in national magazines such as *Horticulture, Fine Gardening, National Gardening, The Herb Quarterly,* and *The Herb Companion.*

C. Colston Burrell is a Master of Landscape Architecture and has an M.S. in horticulture. He is a garden designer, writer, consultant and photographer, and is president of Native Landscape Design and Restoration, Ltd. He coauthored the *Illustrated Encyclopedia of Perennials,* contributed to the *New Encyclopedia of Organic Gardening* and *Landscaping with Nature,* and served as consultant to many gardening books, including *Treasury of Gardening.*

Contents

The Joy of Gardening

The urge to garden, to beautify and enhance one's surroundings by cultivating ornamental or useful plants, is one of humanity's most cherished pastimes and oldest civilized pursuits. Scrolls and wall paintings from Ancient Egypt and vase-paintings from Classical Greece and Rome depict recognizable varieties of flowers grown in pots and borders, demonstrating that the love of green, growing things has been shared by people in many climates and cultures throughout history.

Why do gardens hold this fascination for so many of us? For one thing, many people seem to feel better around plants. Their presence is relaxing and offers an oasis of restful green as an escape from the pressures of everyday life; this phenomenon has even been used in some forms of stress-reduction therapy. In an age when much of life seems to move at an incredibly fast pace and time seems all too short and precious, many people like to feel connected to the slower and gentler rhythms of the natural world. Tilling the soil, planting seeds or young plants, and eagerly awaiting the appearance of new shoots and flowers provides a way for the modern gardener to connect with the processes of nature.

Right: *As soothing to the soul as they are beautiful to the eyes, the flowers and plants in your garden will accent your home and give you a sense of accomplishment.* Above: Monarda didyma.

The making of something beautiful is also its own reward. The word "paradise" derives from the Latin word for garden, paradeisos, and many lovers of flowers and natural greenery consider their own plot a bit of heaven on earth. Gardening is a creative act, and its beauty is in the eye of the beholder. There are as many ideas about what constitutes a fine planting as there are gardeners. A garden can be something as simple as a few seeds hopefully tucked into the soil of a few pots on the kitchen windowsill or as splendid and elaborate as the grounds of Versailles. There are ways of surrounding oneself with fragrant flora for even the tiniest apartment, and for those fortunate enough to own their own patch of earth, there are many styles of gardening and varieties of plants to choose from.

A glance through a few well-illustrated gardening catalogs is enough to set most plant-lovers' dreams spinning elaborate fancies of horticultural heaven. Gardeners are first and foremost eternal optimists, and where there's a will to grow, there's usually a way. While some choose to plant mostly varieties of plants native to their region, others crave the exotic and are drawn toward such pursuits as growing roses in the desert or raising orchids in Manhattan. Most gardeners, and most gardens, fall somewhere in between. No two gardens are ever exactly alike, as they depend for their existence not only upon the necessities of soil, site, and climate, but also upon the personalities, tastes, hopes, and dreams of their creators.

Where, a beginning gardener might ask, ought one to start? Choosing the right style of planting is one place. The best style is one that suits your location and means, satisfies your aesthetic sense, and takes into consideration how you plan to use the garden.

Space need not be the primary concern; it is quite possible to achieve formal effects on a small scale as well as cottage-garden effects on a large scale. Don't feel locked into one style, either; many wonderful effects are achieved by merging styles or creating different looks on different parts of your property. Work with what you like and the results will be sure to be a pleasing expression of your taste, personality, and interests.

An additional consideration lies in how much time you'll have to take care of your garden. Don't plan a labor-intensive scheme for a space you're planning to use solely on weekends, or you're certain to end up doing more weeding than relaxing. In this case, choosing plants and a design that will be fairly low-maintenance will ensure that the time you spend in your garden will be as enjoyable as possible.

Actually sitting down to plan a garden is an exciting prospect. Your first step should be to gather information; if you're going to be successful, you have to know the environment in which you are working. Make an effort to learn what the type of soil is, how much sun the garden receives, and what the drainage is like, so you will be better able to predict what

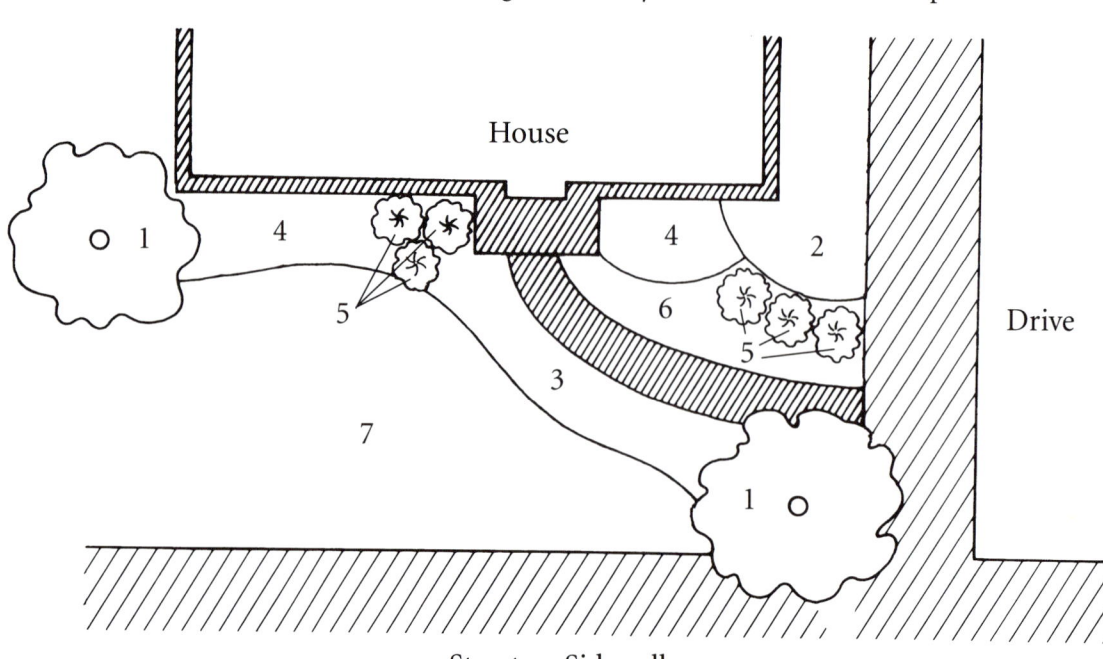

When creating a garden plan for a large area, take into account how the space is used and how the plant life will be viewed, and select and position the various species accordingly.

1 Specimen Shrub or Small Tree
2 Broadleaf Evergreens
3 Low Perennials
4 Medium Perennials or
  Flowering Shrubs
5 Tall Grasses
6 Low Perennials
7 Lawn

House

Drive

Street or Sidewalk

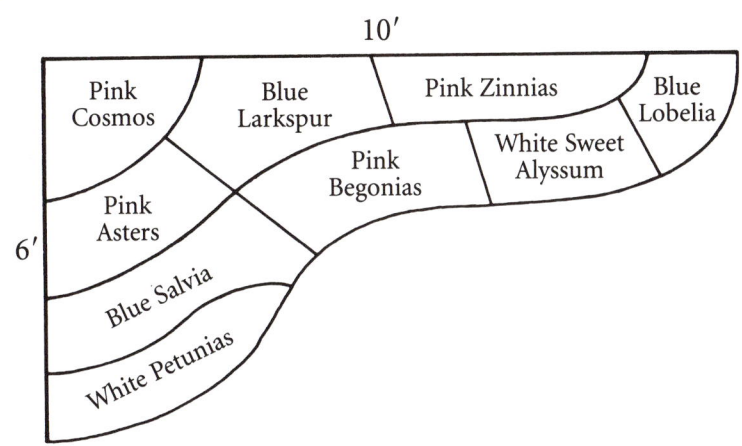

PLANT	HEIGHT	COLOR
Salvia	Medium	Blue
Sweet Alyssum	Low	White
Begonia	Low	Pink
Zinnia	Medium	Pink
Lobelia	Low	Blue
Cosmos	Tall	Pink
Larkspur	Medium	Blue
Aster	Medium	Pink
Petunia	Low	White

When planning a bed of annuals, sketch the desired shape and note the dimensions. Make a list of potential plants, noting their height as well as their color and making sure they are suited to the light, soil, and space available in the bed.

plants will thrive in your garden. With just a little research up front, you will be much better equipped to make planning choices that will lead you to a garden you'll enjoy.

Siting the garden is an important consideration, as the site chosen should suit the type of planting you want to make. For example, planning a rose garden for a shady spot with heavy soil and poor drainage will almost certainly result in a disappointing outcome, but using such a space for astilbe and other plants that have an affinity for damp shade will likely achieve much greater success.

Once you have decided where you want to place the garden and which plants are appropriate for the location you've chosen, actually designing a layout allows you to determine the effect you want to create with the plants you've chosen. This is where stylistic and aesthetic decisions such as formal vs. informal, and mixed plantings vs. carpet bedding or specific plantings (e.g. beds or borders devoted almost solely to roses, hostas, or daylilies) come in. Planning your bedding scheme may be done on plain or gridded paper; there are also garden-planning kits, and now, computer programs that allow you to see how much space you've got and how much room the plants you want to grow will need.

In general, geometric shapes and symmetrical design give a formal effect, while asymmetrically designed plantings and flowing shapes give a more informal effect. Victorian carpet bedding, a formal style, consists of beds planted with differently colored annuals to create a motif or design. This is still often seen in parks, but in the 19th century it was a common scheme for planting in the yards of private homes. In reaction to such stiff formality, new, more naturalistic gardening principles were espoused by such turn-of-the-century experts as Gertrude Jekyll and William Robinson, resulting in the fondness for herbaceous borders (consisting largely of perennials) and mixed borders (containing shrubs, annuals, perennials, and bulbs) that continues today.

Once the garden is planned, you can get into more particulars. Soil preparation is necessary to varying degrees, depending upon your location and on what you want to grow. For most plants, the best soil is a rich, well-drained loam high in decayed organic material such as leaves. However, there are plants suited to every kind of site, and gardens can be made to thrive in everything from very sandy soil (which drains almost instantly and erodes quickly) to heavy clay (which can suffocate roots if not enough air is allowed to get to them).

The pH balance of a soil is a measure of the soil's acidity or alkalinity, which is a prime factor in determining how available its nutrients are to the plants growing there. A pH rating of 6–7 (slightly acid to neutral) is ideal for most garden plants, although some species do prefer to have the soil pH fall above or below this range. Soil test kits are available at most garden centers as well as by mail order, so that the pH of a soil may be determined by the home gardener uncertain about growing conditions.

Adding materials to the soil can help to make it more acid or more alkaline; lime is the primary amendment used to raise pH, while peat moss is one of the most popular choices to help lower it. As the pH of natural compost is usually around 6.5 to 7, adding compost not only helps to enrich soil, but also tends to neutralize pH in cases where it is extremely high or low. Other materials that may be added to soil to help solve various problems include gravel or sand, which break up soil and increase good drainage; topsoil, for areas where this has eroded;

To prepare the ground for planting, first mark off the bed area with pegs and strings. Cut through the sod with a spade and remove the dirt from the bed. Till the area, removing all rocks. Then, spread well-rotted manure, compost, or other soil conditioners to improve soil quality. Finally, rototill or hand dig the bed a second time to thoroughly incorporate these additions and further loosen the soil.

and chemical or natural fertilizers (including compost and manure), which add the elements plants need for healthy growth and plentiful bloom.

The most important thing to remember when actually preparing a bed is to turn over the soil very well, and in the process break up dirt clods and remove invasive grass clumps, roots and all. Turning over increases aeration, which is important, and discourages weeds.

Once the garden is planned out and the soil is prepared, the most exciting part of garden-making begins: filling it up with

plants. There are basically two ways of obtaining plants: growing them from seeds or cuttings, and purchasing already propagated plants from commercial nurseries, either locally or via mail-order. Of course, another good way, once you've got going, is swapping with gardening friends.

Propagating plants isn't as difficult or complicated as it may sound. Many plants will root from cuttings taken with a sharp knife in spring or early summer. Simply pinch off any flower buds and lower leaves, insert the cutting in damp sand or in a mixture of peat moss and perlite, keep it warm and watered, and within the next few weeks to few months it should be rooted. Seeds are generally either started indoors before the growing season begins or planted directly outside in the spot where they are to grow. As with cuttings, keeping them well watered will promote germination.

Plants ordered by mail will arrive either bare-rooted or already growing in a container. While the idea of buying a bare-rooted plant may seem risky, items sent this way aren't any more difficult to handle than those growing in soil. One of the advantages of this method is that you don't have to pay to have the soil shipped in addition to the plant material. Some plants, for instance roses or bulbs, may be shipped in a dormant state. This is nothing to be afraid of and is a part of the natural growth cycle. For any specimens sent through the mail, soak the bare-rooted plants overnight and then plant them in their intended location the next day.

Practicing good maintenance techniques will ensure that the garden you love will keep looking its best. Gardens change all the time, which is one of the loveliest things about them—no garden is the same from year to year because plants grow, mature, die, and are replaced, and annual alterations in weather patterns and seasonal temperatures affect such factors as bloom size, production, and time.

Gardens also change from day to day as new plants start or end their bloom. No matter how small your plot, nothing compares to the excitement of waiting to see a prized perennial blossom that's never bloomed for you before, and then being rewarded for your patience with the bounty of fragrant, colorful flowers.

Maintaining your garden may sound like a chore, but most long-time gardeners find it a pleasure. This is the time to really get to know and get in touch with your plants, to learn the texture and color of the foliage, to observe the intricate beauty of the structure of a flower petal up close, and to indulge your nose in a wide variety of pleasing natural aromas. If you have a cutting garden, while plucking flowers for the house, do a little bit of weeding here and a bit of trimming and tying-up there, and soon the necessary tasks will be done almost before you realize it.

Every garden needs water; how often depends on your area and what you're growing. Some plants, such as those adapted to desert, prairie, or alpine conditions, may be able to exist almost entirely on natural precipitation, while other species need quite a bit of supplemental watering. Fuchsias, for example, are thirsty growers, while rock roses like to be dry; observe your plants to learn their preferences. Note that most container-grown plants dry out more quickly than the same varieties planted directly in the soil, so keep this in mind when doing the rounds.

Watering during the morning or evening hours uses less water than performing this task during the heat of the day, since evaporation is slower when temperatures are cooler. Since

To grow plants from cuttings, first cut 3" to 6" growth tips from the parent plant by making a clean slanted cut. Then, recut the stems just below the bottom node and remove the side shoots and leaves from the lower stems. Dip the lower third of the stems in rooting powder. Poke holes in the rooting medium and insert the cuttings. After 7 to 10 days, check for roots. When the longest roots are ¼" long, transplant them into 1½" pots.

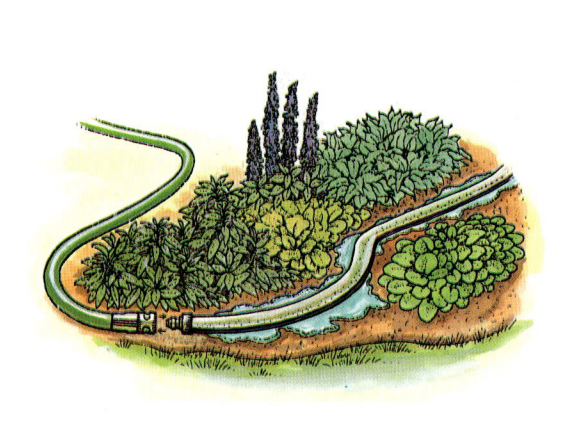

direct sun magnified through water droplets can cause leaf burn, watering at the start or end of the day will also lessen heat stress, which is better for the plants.

Soaker hoses and drip irrigation systems can offer substantial advantages. They benefit the plants by putting water directly onto the soil and root areas where it is needed, and they also will decrease the amount of time and water your garden requires.

Xeriscaping is a time-saving and water-saving technique that utilizes plants with low water requirements to create attractively designed landscape spaces; such areas depend primarily upon natural rainfall, but they may need additional watering during times of extreme drought and when new plants are

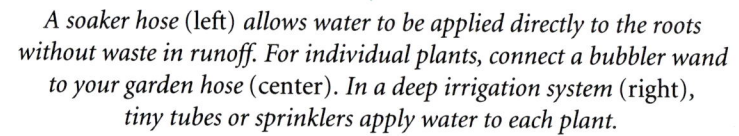

A soaker hose (left) allows water to be applied directly to the roots without waste in runoff. For individual plants, connect a bubbler wand to your garden hose (center). In a deep irrigation system (right), tiny tubes or sprinklers apply water to each plant.

introduced. The moisture requirements of newly transplanted materials are generally higher than those of the same species once established.

Weeding, the subject of so many jokes about gardeners with aching backs, is nonetheless a necessity unless one is content to have a flower bed filled with thistle, dock, and dandelion. Raised beds reduce the wear and tear on the gardener and will benefit those who find bending and pulling a physical difficulty. Sitting on a portable gardening stool while weeding a raised bed helps even more. Knee pads or cushions for kneeling also ease physical demands on knees. Good tools are essential for the task of weeding, as they make the work much easier and more enjoyable; many different varieties of hoes and weeders are offered for sale. Using mulches such as bark chips around the bases of plants helps to discourage weeds from growing, as this greatly cuts down on the amount of sunlight shining directly on the soil and prevents weed seeds and roots from sprouting.

Staking is sometimes necessary for plants whose lush flower heads are too heavy for the stalks to bear without bending and breaking. One of the easiest and most reliable methods for single-stemmed plants such as delphiniums, foxgloves, and lilies is achieved by inserting a wooden or bamboo stake into the ground (being careful not to damage the root systems of any shallow-growing plants) and tying the plant to the stake

In nonmulched plant beds, frequent cultivation of the top few inches of soil is the best way to control weeds. Newly germinated weed seedlings die quickly when stirred up in this way. To control larger weeds, pull them out by hand.

with a double loop. The stake is not obtrusive and adds to rather than detracts from the appearance of the plant, as it allows the blossoms to be displayed to their best advantage. Grow-through hoops are another popular type of support; these are very useful for oriental poppies and other sprawling perennials that tend to have leaves and flowers flopping in every direction. Link stakes are a variation on this theme and are another very good method of tidying up the growth habit of floppy plants, thus making them better border companions.

Grooming can be one of the more pleasant gardening tasks as it may be done in passing. Deadheading, or removing spent flowers, not only improves the appearance of the garden but is also healthy for the plants. Nipping off flowers as they fade prevents photosynthetic energy from going into the formation of seed and may provide the plant with a longer season of bloom.

The simplest form of staking a plant is single staking (left), *in which a stem is secured to a stake that is firmly anchored in the ground. The best way to keep clumps of fine stems upright is to use a stake corral* (center). *Corrals also can be made from L-shaped metal stakes* (right).

Removing yellowing leaves also neatens a plant's appearance and additionally offers the gardener an opportunity to inspect the undersides of leaves for any insect pests. Some leaf drop is normal and is nothing to worry about, but excessive loss of foliage at one time (other than in the autumn) may be an indication of a possible health problem.

Don't over-neaten, however; the yellowing foliage of bulbs such as daffodils and tulips may not have a pleasing appearance, but it needs to remain on the plant until it dies completely to make certain that the bulbs receive enough nutrition from the leaves to flower again the following year. Overplanting

Deadheading should be done soon after the flower dies, so no plant energy is wasted on seed formation. Single flowers should be cut back to the place on the stem where a side shoot is already pushing out. If none is evident, then cut back to above a leaf, a node, or a side branch. Cut on a slant to allow water to run off the wound.

the bulbs with a ground-cover plant will assist in disguising the fading foliage.

Pruning is essential to maintain the health of woody plants such as trees, shrubs, and some vines, and it also keeps the shape of topiary neat and clear. When to prune and whether to do it hard or lightly depends upon the individual plant. Some plants may be successfully pruned at any time of year, while for those that produce bloom on the previous year's growth, such as forsythia and some varieties of clematis, pruning at the wrong time means that the gardener risks losing an entire season of bloom.

With all the possible pests and diseases that can attack plants, it sometimes seems a wonder that any grow healthily. Many useful reference books dealing with the subject in great detail are readily available, some geared toward a specific group of plants or a certain climate zone. As with the health of all living things, an ounce of prevention is worth a pound of cure. Keeping your plants happy by giving them a situation they like, with enough water and sunlight and the proper drainage, and discouraging slugs by keeping the soil fairly free of debris, assists them greatly in fighting off insect pests.

The ongoing management of a garden is a matter of maintaining vigilance, but not strenuously so. One soon cultivates an eye for how a plant should look and can then investigate if something appears to be going amiss. Holes in leaves, little or no flower production, yellowing or curled foliage, and brown spots or edges on leaves are just a few of the possible danger signals. Management quickly becomes second nature, and any gardener who enjoys spending time with his or her plants soon learns what looks right.

Enjoying your garden means choosing a size, style, and plan of care that suit you and your circumstances, and then watching with pleasure as the plants you've chosen and cared for thrive and bloom. For best results, gear your planting toward the way in which you'd like to enjoy it. Don't, for instance, plant island beds of delicate flowers in the middle of a lawn that's often used for play; locate the flower beds instead toward the edges of the lawn to minimize trampling. Plan ahead for seasonal interest, as well—flowers, berries, and attractive foliage are to be had at almost any time of the year. Plant berried or seeding plants for the birds if you want to attract them. Some types of roses set attractive red hips or fruits, which both birds and humans enjoy. Don't overlook fragrance. The scent of roses or honeysuckle drifting on the warm summer air imparts an aspect to garden enjoyment that is at once soothing and romantic. Plan vistas, walks, arbors, or benches, if appropriate to your site, that are conducive to lingering amidst the garden beds and observing individual plants up close. Evening-scented plants and plants light in color are good choices if the primary time you have for enjoying your garden is late in the day. No matter how busy your schedule or difficult your location, there's almost certain to be a gardening technique that's appropriate.

One of the most exciting things about gardening is that it's all up to you. Change things around as much as your heart desires, or find a look you love and stick with it. Small or large, indoors or out, crowded or spare, formal or informal—there's a style that will suit every space, every schedule, and every gardener. Planning and planting gardens opens up a world full of new horizons and new vistas of beauty to explore. Nothing is more pleasant and satisfying than spending time contemplating the beauty you've helped to create. As a gardener, you'll always be able to find something fresh to try and something new to look forward to, and you'll have the assurance that after every bleak and stormy winter there will be a bright spring filled with blossom and birdsong.

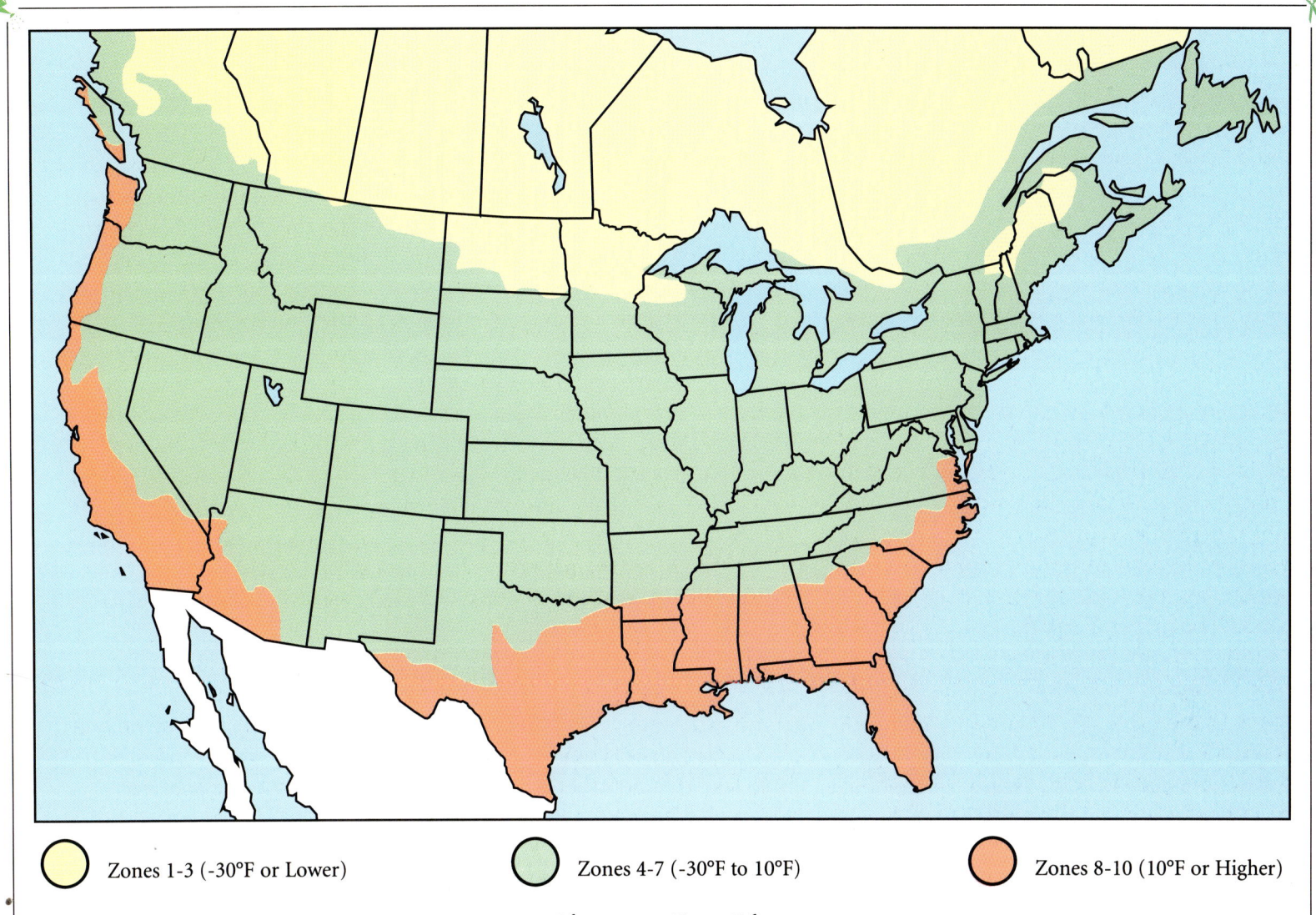

Zones 1-3 (-30°F or Lower)   Zones 4-7 (-30°F to 10°F)   Zones 8-10 (10°F or Higher)

Hardiness Zone Map

Our Hardiness Zone Map is a guide designed to link frost dates with regions. Based on the U.S. Department of Agriculture Plant Hardiness Zone Map, our map collapses the ten zones of the Plant Hardiness Zone Map into three large areas. Zones 1 through 3 are rendered in yellow and represent the coldest areas; Zones 4 through 7 are rendered in green and represent moderate temperatures; Zones 8 through 10 are rendered in orange and represent the warmest zones.

This map offers only a general guideline to temperatures and frost dates. The USDA Plant Hardiness Zone Map is a more thorough approach to depicting temperature zones, but even that map is not perfect. The lines of separation between zones are simply not as clear-cut as any map might depict. Plants recommended for one zone might do well in the southern part of the adjoining colder zone, as well as in the neighboring warmer zone. Factors such as altitude, exposure to wind, and amount of available sunlight also contribute to a plant's winter hardiness. Also note that the indicated temperatures are average minimums—some winters will be colder and others warmer than this figure.

Color Theme Gardens

Many gardens rely on eye-pleasing combinations—either bold or subtle—of various colors of flowers, but the skillful use of only one or two hues can produce some delightful and unusual effects. One of the most well-known single-color gardens was the renowned White Garden planned by Vita Sackville-West at Sissinghurst Castle, but similar borders may be planted on any scale, from large to small. The use of one color or a group of related tones allows the gardener to emphasize the texture and scale of different plants, and also to create some very painterly effects, as Impresssionist painter Claude Monet did in his lovely gardens at Giverny.

As with any garden, color-theme plantings should not be overplanned. Often some of the nicest groupings are the unexpected ones. A splash of yellow from a self-sown seedling, for example, may be just the contrast needed to bring out the full effect of an all-pink or all-blue bedding scheme.

Left: The regular arrangement of the flower beds in this grand white garden allows the eye to perceive subtle tonal differences among the flowers as shades of cream, green, and gray mingle with snowy masses of pure white. Above: Rosa 'Sally Holmes.'

Right: *The glorious tumble of pink and white provided by peonies in full bloom offers a pleasing contrast to the formal geometric shapes of the garden beds themselves, which are inlaid into the turf with almost cookie-cutter precision. Cool gray edging plants and a background of dark green foliage accented by pink and purple climbing roses and clematis help to make this garden a showpiece.*

Left: *Walls can be used as canvases to hold a vertical display of color. Here, vigorously growing climbing roses ('Seven Sisters') in shades of medium pink make a lovely show against mellowed old stone walls, and they frame the window beautifully. At their feet, silver-foliaged plants, including lavender and artemisia, make a cool foil to the spherical heads of allium.*

Opposite page: *Lavender and deep purple pillars of delphinium blooms stand out in this grand-scale garden. White regal lilies and low-growing roses in luscious shades of pink and cream complete the color scheme. A similar effect could be achieved in a much smaller space by re-creating the planting scheme for one of the island beds.*

Right: *An artistic approach to tonal-themed plantings utilizes flower shapes and the growth habits of plants to emphasize the blossom colors. Here, the round flat flower heads of pale yellow* Achillea *'Coronation Gold' contrast with the lush wands of rose-colored bloom borne by* Delphinium *'Astolat,' though both plants share a vertical habit of growth.* Nepeta, oenothera, *and* heuchera *provide a lovely, airy foreground.*

Left: *Ornamental grasses add both color and texture to a planting. In this garden, the feathery, dun-tipped spears make a focal point and add lightness to the rivers of color created by a pink oenothera and several plants of* Dianthus *'Tiny Rubies,' whose foliage colors match the blue-gray of the grass. Though small in scale, the combination is both effective and showy.*

Opposite page: *Twin examples of the classic herbaceous border flow down either side of a narrow grassy path leading to a statue in the shelter of a clipped evergreen. Billowing colors of lavender, blue, pink, rose, and yellow are provided by perennials, including campanula, dame's violet, phlox, dianthus, and achillea. Annuals such as nicotiana are scattered in the mix, and the whole is framed by shrubs and roses.*

Left: *For sheer intensity of color, few flowers can rival the colorful and much-loved zinnia, a cheerful annual that blooms in bright, feisty colors of pink, red, orange, and yellow. In this cozy garden, a double row of mixed zinnias leads to a planting of cooler dark blue larkspur. Bright yellow canvas chairs echo the colors of the flower beds, while the swordlike foliage of irises provides an energetic counterpoint in the small space.*

Right: *Lampranthus, gazanias, and ursinias flaunt their mounds of beautiful daisy-shaped flowers in glowing tones of deep red, bright orange, and pure sunshine gold. With a little thought, mixing several plant species that produce different colors of flowers can create a stunning and dramatic color scheme even when done on a relatively small scale.*

Opposite page: *Warm color accents for the garden are found not only among the ranks of annuals and perennials. Here, trees and shrubs get into the act with both flower and foliage color in an extremely sophisticated and beautifully effective display. Japanese maples provide the backdrop with leaves of deepest plum-red, gold, and chartreuse, while a rhododendron blooming in a rare shade of tangerine bridges the gap between the trees and the perennial bed in front, whose colors of green and gold match those of the maples.*

Right: *A bonny patch of roving black-eyed susans and other free-growing flowers is given structure by a bright white picket fence. The formality of the fence contains and tames the great sheets of sunshine-colored perennials, which give the effect of a wild-flower meadow. The fence also plays up the color of the white phlox, a cool contrast to the otherwise lively color scheme.*

Left: *Even a small space such as this can sustain a fair amount of plant life, and the effect of so much color, texture, and beauty beheld all at once is truly memorable. The unifying color theme of gold, orange, and red tones gives this wonderful combination its aesthetic impact. Plants used include marigolds, lilies, nasturtiums, rudbeckias, chrysanthemums, alstroemerias, and violas.*

Opposite page: *The aptly named Chilean fire bush produces veritable fountains of hot red flowers. Set against a background of darker-foliaged plants and a deep gray stone wall, the branches positively glow. Yellow and red columbines cluster at the base of the woody shrub like sparks scattering from its blaze.*

Right: *Shades of yellow from palest buttercream to deepest gold compose this lovely monochromatic mixed border. Lemon-yellow gladioli and feathery light gold celosia create vertical accents, while the rounded flower forms of nasturtiums, marigolds, and chrysanthemums make a gentle contrast. Ruffled-edged coleus leaves in variegated pale yellow and green provide the perfect foliar complement.*

Left: *The beauty of details can spring to the forefront when the distraction of bold color is removed. Where but in a white garden would the observer notice the pale rosy flush in the throat of white foxgloves, the velvety gray of lambs' ears, the golden centers of ox-eye daisies, or the subtle shade of maroon marking the central cat-face of a pansy?*

Above: *A sea of majestic purple welcomes the visitor to this long border, where the single-color theme is carried out thoroughly. Every flower in sight bears the same imperial shade;* Salvia farinacea, Setcreasa pallida, *and* Artemisia 'Powis Castle' *are some of the contributing plants. Searching out matching shades of bulbs, annuals, perennials, and shrubs can be an enjoyable treasure hunt for the devoted gardener when it yields such splendid results as these.*

Left: *Foliage that echoes the color of the planting scheme can become an integral part of a garden. Here, flowers and leaves together sing a single-color theme in blissful harmony. The snowy chalices of colchicums perfectly match the variegated groundcover foliage, while the frosty silver-gray of fluffy artemisia adds the finishing touch to a scene that is perfection in miniature.*

Opposite page: *Though all-white schemes are often associated with English gardens, this California garden demonstrates that the idea translates extremely well to other locales. The various rounded and spiked habits of the plants contrast very effectively with the simple, square white building with characteristic terra-cotta tile roof in the background. A white garden in a hot climate would be especially nice for use as a moon garden, when temperatures are cooler and white flowers glow in the moonlight.*

Left: *A variation on a single-color theme: Using all-yellow instead of all-white flowers gives an impression of pure sunshine and creates a garden to view by sunlight rather than moonshine. Here, dainty lemon-yellow blooms of Lilium 'Nutmegger' dangle like chandeliers above the multitudinous golden buttons of anthemis.*

Left: *Unexpected combinations can be among the most effective. One might not automatically think of planting copper-colored mums in conjunction with the fuchsia and purple leaves of flowering cabbage, but the center of the mums plays off of the cabbages' color, and the deep jewel tones of both plants make a rich and lovely pairing. Experimentation can lead to some wonderful, serendipitous discoveries.*

Right: *Creamy pale nasturtiums float like butterflies over their own rounded leaves, which seem to bring to mind floating water lilies. The combination of the blooming nasturtiums and the tiny gold-netted leaves of a variegated Japanese honeysuckle makes this planting a gilded treasure where the fine lines of the foliage echo the pale hue of the petals.*

Opposite page: *This large-scale planting incorporates variegated shrubs as a backdrop to a lush planting of gleamingly colored annuals, perennials, and bulbs. The occasional touches of red flowers and bronze foliage help to bring out the gilded colors of the main part of the planting, as do the darker green trees at the end of the vista.*

Opposite page: *In a setting worthy of their name and of their beauty, lovely regal lilies fill a raised stone bed with floral bounty. The colors of this planting have been chosen with great care: White peonies and daisies in the border beyond echo the snowy, gold-centered throats of the lilies, while pink roses match the blush of color striping the outside of each pale trumpet.*

Right: *The combination of three very different flowers in similar shades effectively draws attention to both the form and color of the plants. Though all bloom in like tones of rosy lavender, the rounded globes of* Allium grandis, *the spires of* Lythrum *'Morden's Pink,' and the clustered rosettes of* Rosa *'Baby Faurax' differ greatly in texture and outline.*

Left: *A symphony in shades of pink and purple carries the theme from nearly white, through a wide range of pastels, to deep magenta. The centerpiece for this lush, gorgeous border is a collection of hybrid foxgloves in a vast range of complementary tones. The weathered blue-gray of the wooden fence underscores the blue tones of the flowers and repeats in its shape the serried ranks of the foxgloves. Obedient plant and phlox in various shades of pink form the foreground.*

ACHILLEA FILIPENDULINA
FERNLEAF YARROW
PERENNIAL; HARDY TO ZONE 2

This yarrow bears 4″ flat flower heads in delicate shades of yellow or gold that rest atop tall stems with finely cut foliage in late summer. A position in the middle to the back of the perennial border shows off the stature of this sun-lover.

ALLIUM GIGANTEUM
FLOWERING ONION
BULB; HARDY TO ZONE 5

This summer-blooming bulb is a standout for its enormous globes of purple flowers carried on tall, sturdy stems. The flowers cut and dry well, but the plant may have an oniony smell. It grows well in full sun to part shade.

ANTHEMIS TINCTORIA
GOLDEN MARGUERITE
PERENNIAL; HARDY TO ZONE 3

A profusion of golden-yellow, daisylike flowers are produced over the delicate foliage of this plant from May to July. Though the individual flowers are small, they are produced in large quantities. Either full sun or part shade will do.

ARTEMISIA 'POWIS CASTLE'
PERENNIAL; HARDY TO ZONE 5

Valued for its ornamental leaves rather than its flowers, this cultivar produces mounds of lacy silver foliage all summer; it withstands sun and winds but must have good drainage as the roots rot in wet soil.

ASTER NOVI-BELGII HYBRIDS AND CULTIVARS
MICHAELMAS DAISY
PERENNIAL; MOST HARDY TO ZONE 3

Daisylike flowers in harmonious shades of blue, rose, and purple will bloom from late summer to fall, depending upon the cultivar chosen. A range of plant heights (1–4′) allows for varied use within a design. They tend to spread and so require extra attention in formal plantings.

BRASSICA OLERACEA ACEPHALA GROUP
FLOWERING KALE
BIENNIAL; USED AS AN ANNUAL

This vegetable's large leafy rosettes of medium to dark green with a white, pink, or red center make a bold color statement. The plants may be easily grown from seed and are good in pots. Potted plants may be used as indoor decoration and are good for fall bedding-out schemes.

CAMPANULA LACTIFLORA
MILKY BELLFLOWER
PERENNIAL; HARDY TO ZONE 3

Clusters of bell-shaped, pink, white, blue, or violet flowers bloom at the top of slender, arching 3–4′ stems in June and July. A good plant for naturalizing, it will self-sow. Full sun to part shade and a moist, rich soil are best.

CHRYSANTHEMUM X MORIFOLIUM
FLORISTS' CHRYSANTHEMUM
PERENNIAL; HARDINESS VARIES

These classic staples for the autumn garden bear very showy flowers in a myriad of sizes, forms, and colors, usually from midsummer to frost. Plants enjoy sun and adequate water; the flowers are excellent for cutting and create a bold display of color in either garden or vase.

DAHLIA HYBRIDS
DAHLIA
TUBER; NOT HARDY

Dahlia's bright, clear colors and symmetrical blossoms will enhance a warm-colored border. Dig the tubers in fall after frost and store them in bags of peat for the winter, replanting in spring. Available in a wide variety of colors, heights, and flower shapes, some dahlias also do well in pots.

DIGITALIS PURPUREA
FOXGLOVE
BIENNIAL; HARDY TO ZONE 4

Beautiful spikes of tubular flowers with attractively spotted throats appear from May through September and will enhance any cool-colored or pastel planting scheme. They love dappled shade and moist soil, and may self-sow. The plants are poisonous if ingested.

GYPSOPHILA PANICULATA
BABY'S BREATH
PERENNIAL; HARDY TO ZONE 4

Sizeable clouds of tiny single or double white blooms appear from May to July; the plants may grow 3–4′ tall and just as wide. It makes a wonderful companion for pink roses and blue campanulas or delphiniums. A classic for cutting and drying.

HEUCHERA HYBRIDS
CORAL BELLS
PERENNIAL; HARDY TO ZONE 3

Sprays of tiny pink, scarlet, or white flowers appear from May to June over clumps of scalloped leaves, which are attractively veined or variegated in some varieties. At 8–12″ tall, this is a good plant for edging. A variety of conditions suits these versatile and dainty plants.

IRIS SIBERICA
SIBERIAN IRIS
PERENNIAL; HARDY TO ZONE 3

Blue, violet, or white flowers, sometimes with darker veining, make an attractive show in June. An excellent choice for the blue or white garden, they stand about 30″ tall, make good cut flowers, and occasionally re-bloom. They like a moist soil and a partly sunny situation.

ROSA SHRUB ROSE TYPES
SHRUB; MOST HARDY TO ZONE 5

Generally, shrub roses have smaller-sized blooms than do hybrid teas, but they bear them in far greater quantities; they are wonderful for adding a waterfall of color to a fence or garden corner. Many colors and cultivars are available. All prefer several hours of sun daily and good drainage.

SALVIA SUPERBA/NEMOROSA
FLOWERING SAGE
PERENNIAL; HARDY TO ZONE 4

These shrubby salvias display their plentiful wands of tiny blue, lavender, or pink flowers during June and July. They are excellent for adding a dash of cool color to a sunny border. The foliage is aromatic, and the flowers are good for cutting.

STACHYS LANATA
LAMBS' EARS
PERENNIAL; HARDY TO ZONE 4

Spires of tiny rose-lavender flowers come in early summer, but this plant is loved for its rosettes of furry, oval, silver-gray leaves. It's an excellent way to add a splash of color to a white border. Lambs' ears likes part shade and good drainage, and it will spread.

Cottage Gardens

Cottage gardens appeal to the romantic in all of us. Their generous variety of plants growing together in a relatively small space speaks of bounty and life, and the overall look reminds us of a simpler, gentler time. The cottage garden design was splendidly captured in the beautiful watercolors of the artist Helen Allingham; her pictures of roses growing around the doors of lovingly maintained thatched cottages and small flower gardens bursting with colorful blossoms are still part of our image of the ideal cottage garden today.

Cottage gardening is a wonderful way to manage many different plant types in a small space, since the typical cottage garden displays annuals, perennials, herbs, shrubs, and vegetables, all growing quite happily together with an effect of controlled chaos. With cottage gardening, even a rooftop garden in an urban setting can have a refreshing feel of the country.

Right: The well-defined, curved shape of the beds and the stepping stones leading to a paved area help to tame the abundance of bloom in this thriving cottage yard. A free-standing urn repeats in miniature both the colors and the style of its surroundings. Above: Clematis 'Carnaby.'

Opposite page: *Golden laburnums drop long panicles of bloom from overhead in this bowerlike allée planting, while from underneath, the pale lavender globes of* Allium aflatuense *rise to meet them. The wooden support blends in appearance with the trunks of the laburnum trees, thus calling more attention to the plants themselves. This lovely and timeless vista ends, appropriately, at a sundial.*

Right: *Rambling pink roses and other climbers are trained over a rustic wooden pergola; this type of trellis would give a country-cottage feel to a garden even if it were set in the midst of a bustling city. Warm salmon-pink poppies and large, medium-green hosta leaves make a bold showing in the foreground, complementing the light and airy feel of the pergola.*

Opposite page: *A splendidly thriving 'Lady Banks' rose proffers cascades of sweetly scented, fluffy yellow blooms that glow like sunshine even on the cloudiest day. The pale wooden arbor harmonizes nicely with the white clapboard house and with the gray gravel path outlined in warmer red brick. A wide variety of plants blooming in luscious pastel tones, including tulips, rhododendrons, pansies, and primroses, round off a lovely spring display.*

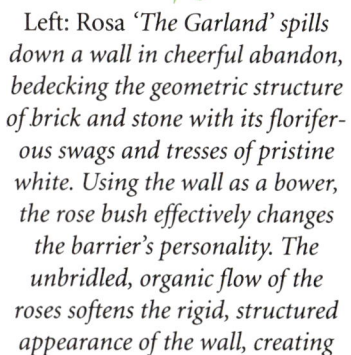

Left: Rosa *'The Garland' spills down a wall in cheerful abandon, bedecking the geometric structure of brick and stone with its floriferous swags and tresses of pristine white. Using the wall as a bower, the rose bush effectively changes the barrier's personality. The unbridled, organic flow of the roses softens the rigid, structured appearance of the wall, creating a welcoming approach to the garden beyond.*

Right: *Another brick-and-stone wall has been given a more designed planting, for a different but no less charming effect. Espaliered flowering quinces have been trained against the wall in a fan pattern, while brightly colored primroses fill the beds at their feet. Fruit trees may also be trained in espalier fashion; the warmth of the wall allows fruit to ripen more quickly and flowers to open earlier than they otherwise would.*

Opposite page: *The quintessential cottage surely has a thatched roof and roses growing around the door; this lovely scene fulfills those requirements and makes a perfect picture. Exuberant perennial beds stretch from right below the windows out onto the lawn, while other plantings cluster around the rough front gate. An ornamental sedge in the foreground and a wheelbarrow-shaped planter sporting mixed annuals add distinctive touches to a classic look.*

Left: *Using a vertical approach to gardening allows for the maximum show of bloom in any space, large or small. In this mature California planting, a relatively large space has been filled with magenta bougainvillea and flame-colored lantana, which are covering a wall and stairway alcove with brightly tinted blossoms and bracts. Underplantings echo the hot colors of the taller shrubs and vines.*

Right: *The riot of color provided by lilies, dahlias, and other tall-growing bulbs and perennials is bordered by a white picket fence in the front and dark evergreens and deciduous trees behind in the yard of a quiet-toned historic homestead. This lively planting demonstrates one of the most useful techniques of cottage garden design: combining bright, informally growing flowers with a controlling element such as a fence or formal garden bed.*

Left: *A white picket fence and gray-shingled house show off a sterling example of the New England dooryard garden, a cottage garden subtype. The brick walk and well-tended mixed plantings on either side are other characteristic features. White roses, pale yellow* Achillea *'Moonshine,' and fuzzy gray lambs' ears are featured among the plantings, which also include an assortment of shrubs and trees.*

Opposite page: *Gardens that emphasize their regions' traditional styles of architecture and design have special charm. The flavor of the southeastern United States is caught in this front garden with its elaborate wrought iron balcony, beautiful as a black lace mantilla. Azaleas in pink and white, rows of potted geraniums, and a windmill palm also grace the scene.*

Left: *A symphony in restful sea-greens is provided by this mix of herbs, shrubs, and perennials, whose color scheme, but not planting style, is unusual. Showy foliage plants in colors ranging from blue to chartreuse, feathery fennel, and euphorbia with pale yellow helianthemum thrive in a sunny corner against a pure white wall, giving the effect of Californian lushness.*

 These two gorgeous examples wonderfully illustrate the inventive use of containers. In one (above), *a selection of plants in pinks, whites, and greens, including agapanthus, verbena, lychnis, and boxwood, is clustered in front of a border of blooming hydrangeas and taller evergreens. In the other* (right), *a bounty of potted geraniums, petunias, lobelias, and other flowers, with red predominating, are hung at different heights, allowing each pot its maximum visual impact while creating a floral screen for the porch.*

Left: *A glorious combination of formal and informal elements, this garden truly makes the most of its allotted space. Twin standard bay trees with floral underplanting flank the front door, while paired containers hosting a variety of blooms are placed at intervals down the steps of the porch. In the front garden, poppies, foxgloves, lychnis, and lilies are given free rein, and an out-of-bloom wisteria vine clothes a wall with its abundance of verdure.*

Left: *Plum, rose, green, and gold burst forth as the main colors in this small square bed, but the use of the deep plum color unexpectedly comes from dark-leaved shrubs. In this lively planting, the towering poppies are supported by an underplanting of mixed perennials. Tiny heartsease are set directly in front of the central dark shrub, using it as a perfect background for their dainty blossoms. The plum, green, and gold are repeated in the colors of the larger-scale background border.*

Opposite page: *Neatly trimmed boxwood is no match for the abundant growth of the lime-colored alchemilla, which flows right over the clipped hedge in what seems to be an excess of pure joie de vivre. Brilliant crimson lobelia and peonies back up the cheerful spirit of the alchemilla in this lushly growing border, containing a wide variety of mixed shrubs and perennials.*

Left: *Even in harsh winter, exuberant growth finds a way to assert itself. Here, frost has touched an urn-planted helichrysum to create a graceful picture of silver perfection. The border plants have likewise been given a generous dusting of sparkling white, and even the cracks between the paving stones are outlined with ice crystals.*

Right: This winding walkway with its attendant overflowing garden beds creates an air of mystery about the little gazebo at its end. The curving shape of the path prevents a clear line of vision, and the careful groupings of unabashed perennials help to further obscure parts of the structure from view. The visitor is thus enticed to wander down the meandering trail to see what floral surprises await and what further promising vistas beckon.

Right: *Flourishing phlox and black-eyed susans are grown in wide, bold swathes in this coastal Maine garden, creating a sunny, artistic, and undeniably vibrant vision of life in flower. The sprawling apple tree, simple picket fence, and inviting stretch of meadow beyond complete a perfect country landscape picture.*

Left: *A central patch of emerald-green lawn is surrounded by beds abundantly planted with foxtail lilies, peonies, phlox, poppies, and evening primroses, which in turn are backed by shrubs and then taller trees. The gradual increase in height of the background plantings screens such mundane articles as telephone lines and buildings from view, so that they do not intrude on the isolated, enchanted atmosphere of this gladelike lawn and garden.*

Opposite page: *Many cottage gardens contain areas of flowers planted purely for cutting. The broad swathes of color they display make attractive sights in their own right; like the rest of the typical cottage garden, cutting areas are planted with an eye to both function and beauty. The selections shown here, which include* Salvia farinacea, Gomphrena globosa, *and cockscomb, are excellent for both fresh and dried bouquets.*

Right: *This bountiful cutting garden spreads out its colorful array on a hillside in the mid-morning sunshine. Thriving astilbe, coreopsis, salvia, digitalis, and chrysanthemum mean that summer vases need never go unfilled. Though this garden is rather grand in scale, a smaller sunny space planted with flowers for cutting would also allow for the creation of many cheerful homegrown bouquets.*

Above: *Rosy-purple liatris and pale-yellow achillea are a subtle combination that shows well against the taupe background of the house and will provide material for cutting should the gardener so desire. The tall feathery plumes of an ornamental grass echo both the color and the vertical lines of the house's architecture, while another ornamental grass forms blue-gray rosettes for the edging in the foreground.*

Left: *Useful gardening is possible even in the smallest of spaces. Here an herb garden in miniature flourishes delightfully in a terra-cotta strawberry pot, providing fresh chives, mint, and parsley as condiments for the table. The nasturtium and the rambunctious vines of perennial pea growing at right repeat the abundance of the herb pot on a larger scale, while the lavender pea flowers match the color of the chive blossoms.*

Right: *Many kitchen-garden plants could be grown for their visual appeal rather than for table use alone. The beautiful shiny bronze and green leaves of this Swiss chard are accented by ruby veins, creating a contrast to the flat blue of the broccoli leaves behind, while a showy variegated nasturtium twines around both, displaying its crimson and gold blossoms above white-marbled foliage. Though often grown as ornamentals, nasturtium flowers and foliage are edible (as long as they have not been sprayed for insects) and add a peppery taste to salads.*

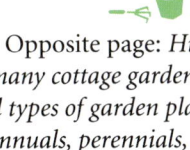

Opposite page: *Historically, many cottage gardens combined all types of garden plants together: annuals, perennials, bulbs, trees, shrubs, herbs, and even fruits and vegetables. Taking a leaf or two from this tradition, modern gardeners can practice companion planting—combining disparate sorts of plants that grow well together—and make even the working parts of gardens beautiful as well as useful. This excellent example arranges its vegetables in neat geometric beds with growing frames, while shrubs, vines, and a large trellis provide aesthetic accents.*

ALCHEMILLA MOLLIS
LADY'S MANTLE
PERENNIAL; HARDY TO ZONE 4

Profuse, fluffy clusters of tiny, chartreuse flowers appear on this cottage garden favorite in May and June. The sea-green leaves have a pleated appearance when young and tend to hold drops of dew and water, giving them a silvery look. A cool, moist, lightly shaded situation is best.

ALLIUM SCHOENOPRASUM
CHIVES
BULB; HARDY TO ZONE 2

Small, round flower heads, usually rose-colored, appear in summer, but the real attractions are the 6″ grasslike leaves that can be used as a seasoning. Chives will spread rapidly, so be prepared to divide or contain them.

ASTILBE X ARENDSII HYBRIDS
PERENNIAL; HARDY TO ZONE 3

Planting a combination of astilbe varieties can give you a prolific display of the plumelike flowers from early summer to late fall, in soft shades of pink, red, rose, and cream. This easy-to-please perennial enjoys a moist environment and will bloom in either sun or shade.

BAPTISIA AUSTRALIS
FALSE INDIGO
PERENNIAL; HARDY TO ZONE 3

This hardy, attractive, and practically trouble-free plant has spires of intensely blue flowers in June and July, followed by black seed pods that are also quite ornamental. The long-lived plants are 3–4′ tall and prefer good drainage.

BETA VULGARIS CICLA GROUP
RUBY CHARD
BIENNIAL; GROWN AS AN ANNUAL

These members of the beet family are grown for their ornamental foliage. Puckered, dark green leaves with contrasting bright magenta stems and veins make them a perfect choice for gardeners wishing to re-create some of the traditional cottage garden vegetable-and-flower combinations.

BOUGAINVILLEA X BUTTIANA
BOUGAINVILLEA
PERENNIAL VINE; HARDY TO ZONE 8

This glorious deciduous vine sprouts tiny flowers surrounded by showy bracts in pink, red, white, purple, or yellow. It grows vigorously in southern and western areas, flowering in spring and summer, and makes an excellent conservatory climber in colder regions. Full sun and dry soil suit it best.

CELOSIA HYBRIDS
ANNUAL

This old-fashioned annual comes in many varieties and produces feathery or crested flower heads, usually colored red, yellow, orange, or pink. Seeds may be sown indoors before planting, or started plants may be purchased; most varieties will do well in pots. The plants are 8–24″ tall and like full sun.

CHRYSANTHEMUM X SUPERBUM
SHASTA DAISY
PERENNIAL; HARDY TO ZONE 3

This plant does not like overly hot or dry conditions, but appreciates at least half a day of sun. At 2–3′ tall, it's an excellent plant for the middle of the border, and the classic daisy flowers make a wonderful addition to a fresh bouquet.

CLEMATIS HYBRIDS
PERENNIAL VINE; HARDY TO ZONE 3

The flowers of most clematis hybrids are large, star-shaped, single or double blooms in shades of red, pink, purple, blue, and white. Some varieties of the vine grow to 15′ but may be trimmed back. Many tolerate shade, and all are good for growing through shrubs.

COSMOS BIPINNATUS
COSMOS
ANNUAL

Cosmos are very easily grown from seed; sow in place after the last frost in spring. The large flowers boast broad petals in pink, white, or red rising on wiry 4′ stems. Good for the back of the border, it likes a sunny spot and is a traditional choice for a cut flower.

DELPHINIUM HYBRIDS
PERENNIAL; HARDY TO ZONE 3

The spectacular blue, purple, and white spires of delphinium hybrids appear in profusion in June, making a garden focal point. A second, smaller flush of bloom may follow in September. With 2–5′ stalks, the plants often need staking, and they like abundant sun, water, and fertilizer.

GERANIUM 'JOHNSON'S BLUE'
PERENNIAL; HARDY TO ZONE 4

Small but attractive cup-shaped flowers are carried on 15″ stems over the lobed, medium-green leaves from June through August. Full sun to light shade is best. This plant is not fussy about soil; it spreads but is easily divided.

GLADIOLUS X HORTULANUS
GLADIOLUS; SWORD LILY
CORM; HARDY TO ZONE 8

These showy summer-bloomers like sun and can easily be grown in cold climates if they are lifted in the fall and replanted in spring. Flowers bloom in a wide range of colors and bicolors, and the sword-shaped leaves are also attractive.

GOMPHRENA GLOBOSA
GLOBE AMARANTH
ANNUAL

Attractive pink, white, or purple flowers with the appearance of large, papery clover blossoms are borne several to each 6″ stem in summer. This drought-tolerant plant loves full sun and may be grown from seed or from started plants.

LACTUCA SPECIES
LEAF LETTUCE
ANNUAL

The compact, bright green rosettes of leaf lettuce hybrids form an attractive edging to a vegetable garden, herb garden, or mixed planting. The leaves are delicious when used in sandwiches and salads as well. Leaf lettuce likes sun and water, and can be raised from seed or started plants.

LANTANA CAMARA
LANTANA
SHRUB; HARDY TO ZONE 8

Where hardy, lantanas can be used for ground cover or as small hedges; elsewhere they may be grown in hanging baskets and treated as annuals or wintered indoors. Showy flowers in orange, pink, and yellow cluster at the end of the long stems in summer. Full sun promotes prolific blooming.

LIATRIS SPICATA
GAYFEATHER
PERENNIAL; HARDY TO ZONE 3

Purple or white spikes of flowers are the hallmark of this North American native species. The 2–3′ flower spikes bloom in July and August and are terrific for naturalizing and cutting. Sun or part shade is best for this attractive wildflower; it dislikes clay soil.

LILIUM ASIATIC HYBRIDS
BULB; HARDY TO ZONE 5

A gallery of choices exists for color, height, and bloom season among these garden bulbs. They will do well in ground cover, as the bulbs need shade and the foliage wants at least half a day of sun. The star-shaped flowers are wonderful in arrangements.

LONICERA SEMPERVIRENS
TRUMPET HONEYSUCKLE
PERENNIAL VINE; HARDY TO ZONE 4

Red or reddish-orange tubular flowers are borne in whorls at the ends of long vine branches in summer; the branches may reach 24′. Though this species is not fragrant, honeysuckles have long been a favorite cottage garden plant. They are happy in either sun or part shade.

LYCHNIS CORONARIA
ROSE CAMPION
PERENNIAL; HARDY TO ZONE 4

Bright magenta flowers on 2′ stalks make a lively combination with the plant's grayish, woolly foliage. This simple but eye-catching plant likes sun and is drought tolerant. Popular in English gardens as long ago as 1597, this classic garden plant makes a good cut flower.

MONARDA DIDYMA
BEE BALM; BERGAMOT; OSWEGO TEA
PERENNIAL; HARDY TO ZONE 3

The distinctive mop-headed flower clusters of this North American native are loved by bees as well as by humans. Full sun to part shade is best, and the plant likes an evenly moist soil. This species naturalizes well and may become somewhat invasive.

PAEONIA SUFFRUTICOSA
TREE PEONY
DECIDUOUS SHRUB; HARDY TO ZONE 5

These elegant, upright shrubs produce spectacular cupped blossoms in early summer in shades including red, pink, yellow, and white, sometimes with a poppy-like dark blotch at the base of the petals. The shrubs may grow to 7′ tall and as wide, but may be kept smaller by selective pruning.

PAPAVER ORIENTALE
ORIENTAL POPPY
PERENNIAL; HARDY TO ZONE 3

The crinkled red, pink, or white blossoms of oriental poppies are accompanied by long, attractive toothed leaves. These large plants have a lax habit of growth, and the 2–4′ stems sometimes need support. Oriental poppies are best grown in full sun. Attractive seed heads follow the flowers.

PETROSELINUM CRISPUM
PARSLEY
BIENNIAL; GROWN AS ANNUAL

This culinary herb, with its crisply curled, medium-green leaves, is easily grown from seed and is an attractive garden plant as well. A good choice for mixed flower and herb plantings, it prefers full sun to part shade, and it may also be grown in pots.

Petunia Trailing Hybrids
Perennial; Grown as Annual

Petunias are actually perennials, but they are not winter-hardy and so are usually grown as annual bedding plants. Classic, versatile plants, they are good in pots, hanging baskets, borders, and beds. White cultivars often have blooms that are fragrant, especially at night.

Rosa Climbers and Ramblers
Rose
Shrubs; Many Hardy to Zone 4

The long, pliant branches of rambling roses bear bunches of fragrant flowers in June. Some types bloom until frost. Most are excellent choices for growing on walls, trellises, or fences. Red, pink, white, mauve, and yellow varieties are available.

Salvia Farinacea
Flowering Sage
Perennial; Hardy to Zone 8

As this salvia is not hardy in colder areas, it is usually grown as an annual bedding plant. Graceful, slender spikes of blue flowers bloom from summer to fall on a plant that sometimes grows up to 2′ tall and as wide. Full sun is best.

Tagetes Erecta/Patula
African and French Marigolds
Annuals

African and French marigolds are excellent summer bedding plants that bloom in shades of yellow, gold, and orange from June to frost. African marigolds are taller and have large rounded flowers; French marigolds are excellent pot and edging plants with smaller blooms.

Tropaeolum Majus
Nasturtium
Annual

This trailing plant blooms from July to September in summery tones of red, orange, cream, yellow, and gold. The peppery flowers and leaves are edible if not sprayed. Full sun and little fertilizer create the optimum blooming and growing conditions.

Tulipa Lily
Tulip
Bulb; Hardy to Zone 3

The chalice-shaped blooms of tulips emerge in a rainbow of shades in April and May to gladden the hearts of gardeners. The lily-flowered varieties have unusual, elegant blossoms with pointed, reflexed petals. All tulips thrive in a sunny spot with good drainage.

Valeriana Officinalis
Valerian; Garden Heliotrope
Perennial; Hardy to Zone 3

Attractive, flat inflorescences consisting of many tiny pink, mauve, or white fragrant flowers bloom at the end of 3′ tall stalks in summer. The basal clump of deep-clefted, lance-shaped leaves is also attractive. Valerian may need staking and grows best in full sun to part shade.

Zinnia Elegans
Zinnia
Annual

These Mexican natives bear colorful flowers in bright shades of pink, red, white, yellow, and orange all summer until frost. Standard varieties are about 18″ tall; dwarf varieties are good in pots and for edging. Zinnias love a well-drained soil with adequate watering in full sun.

Country Gardens

The English country look relies on a pleasing combination of formality and informality that uses tastefully planned color schemes and artwork as a counterpoint. An English country garden might contain a formal carpet bed, an avenue of pleached limes, an ornamental pond and fountain, and a well-filled perennial border. Often statuary, containers, or other ornaments are used to offset the garden plan. Though the idea may sound grand, it may also be scaled down. A mixed planting of bulbs, annuals, and perennials surrounding a sundial or birdbath flanked by a pair of rose trees would make a lovely display that requires only the smallest of spaces.

By contrast, the American country garden bespeaks the lush informality of a meadow filled with wildflowers. Often a mixture of grasses, shrubs, annuals, perennials, bulbs, and native plants, the American country garden may also be scaled down; a gathering of daffodils or shasta daisies blooming beside a fence or doorway is as appropriate to classic country style as is an entire sunny meadow of blossoming beauty.

Right: *The blue-green rosette of each 'Lyssako' cabbage opens to reveal a fuchsia heart, creating a striking, wild effect among the rigidly planted beds, strict herb borders, and precise gravel walks of this formal garden.* Above: Brassica oleracea.

Right: *For some, the traditional English country garden represents the apogee of botanical loveliness. Instead of dotting isolated specimens of different species throughout the border, large numbers of one variety of plant are grouped together, allowing the delightful color harmonies to be appreciated from afar as well as amidst the plantings themselves. Coral-pink poppies are a standout in this border; other species include gypsophila, dianthus, delphinium, and penstemon.*

Opposite page: *A blaze of ruffled scarlet peonies provides the centerpiece for this long herbaceous border. Echoing the color principles of Gertrude Jekyll, the length of the border is emphasized by placing the bright, hot colors of the peony, mauve dianthus, and crimson penstemon toward the middle of the border, while placing the cooler colors of the fluffy chartreuse alchemilla toward the end.*

Left: *Eighteenth-century elegance still thrives among the restored buildings, brick pathways, and white picket fences of Colonial Williamsburg, Virginia; American gardens during that era took their cue from the formality prevailing in the gardens of England and France. Forget-me-nots here give a dainty azure edging to rectangular beds planted thickly with spring favorites such as tulip, wild columbine, bleeding heart, and basket-of-gold alyssum.*

Using purple as the primary color, these two gardens bring together a great many species. A richly overflowing border of country flowers presents drifts of bloom in variations on the lavender shade (below), *while a more formal garden backed by a stone wall adds sparkle to the theme with the addition of yellow and white* (right). *Generous numbers of liatris, anemone, and phlox appear in the former, while the latter boasts perennials including platycodon, Shasta daisy, achillea, veronica, and astilbe.*

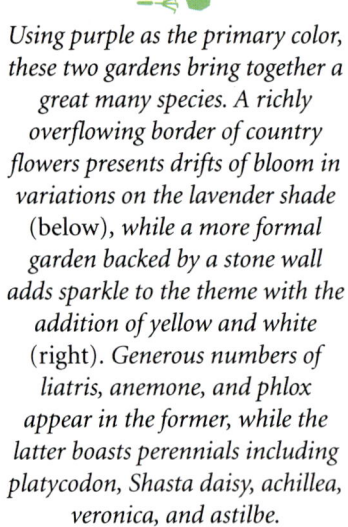

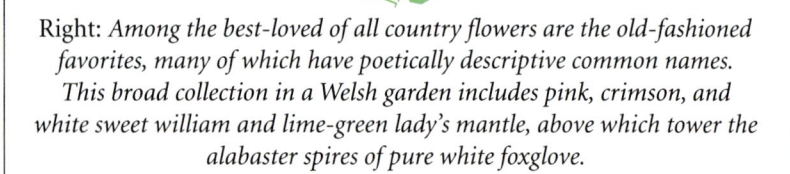

Right: *Among the best-loved of all country flowers are the old-fashioned favorites, many of which have poetically descriptive common names. This broad collection in a Welsh garden includes pink, crimson, and white sweet william and lime-green lady's mantle, above which tower the alabaster spires of pure white foxglove.*

Left: *This picture-perfect garden, looking like an illustration from a Beatrix Potter tale, features Alice-in-Wonderland style standard roses. The rest of the herbaceous border, planted in painterly hues of rich scarlet, royal purple, and white, features* Iris x germanica, peony, aubretia, and dame's violet (Hesperis matronalis).

Right: *"England is a garden that is full of stately views," wrote Rudyard Kipling, and though this particular view is located in Chicago, it demonstrates that the mixed-planting principles of traditional English-style gardening may be applied in many different locales. Perennials including liatris, white coneflower, yarrow, and veronica mingle with annual cosmos, pansies, and zinnias and offer ample material for fresh bouquets.*

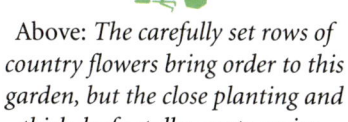

Above: *The carefully set rows of country flowers bring order to this garden, but the close planting and thick, leafy stalks create an impression of natural, untended growth at the same time. This rustic, heavily planted composition gives equal weight to annuals, perennials, and grasses, including rudbeckia, eupatorium, pennisetum, verbena, and perovskia.*

Left: *The widespread interest in horticulture and botany during the nineteenth century led to the practice of mixing tropical exotics with more familiar annuals, shrubs, and perennials. Tall-flowering cannas such as these, brought to England from India during the heyday of the British Empire, are now familiar to gardeners all over the world. Cannas and other tropical plants are tender and should be lifted in the autumn and kept indoors until spring, when they can be replanted.*

Right: *The practice of creating patterns on the ground with botanical material originated with the Elizabethans and their knot gardens of clipped herbs or shrubs, but the Victorians expanded the idea by using colorful annual flowers to create the popular carpet bedding designs of the era. In this composition, swirls of lilac, gold, and white are formed by bedded-out pansies in the foreground, while yellow tulips and pink and white dogwood complete the background picture.*

Left: *This design—outlines of clipped herbs with the spaces between filled with bedding annuals—combines the effect of a knot garden with carpet bedding. The bright combination of purple and red flowers is toned down by the cooler silver and blue-green tones contributed by the herb foliage. A similar arrangement could easily be adapted for a front-yard planting.*

Right: *The most frequently seen use of large-scale contemporary carpet bedding is in public parks, where garden and greenhouse space allow for growing and planting many flats of annuals on a yearly basis. A design similar to the one seen here could easily be adapted to the smaller scale of the home garden and planted in like manner with yellow and tangerine French marigolds and scarlet petunias, combined with contrasting silver dusty miller.*

Right: *Garden ornaments have long been a welcome feature of country gardens. Art in the garden can make a very effective outdoor focal point, displaying one type of artistry against another. Here, the sinuous forms of the crane statuary are echoed in the weeping branches of blue Atlas cedar and the uplifted purple spires of salvia. Gray stone steps and bright green boxwood complete the contemplative scene.*

 Above: *Any garden will benefit from a few ornaments and witty surprises. An unexpected human form among the greenery appears in the shape of this friendly statue, which appears to wave a greeting to the viewer from amongst the coneflower, cleome, and sedum. Lacking the solemnity of more formal sculpture, this example seems to have hopped down from its pedestal to gather a country nosegay in an excess of high spirits.*

Left: *Sundials have been beloved garden features for centuries in both grand gardens and small, long after the need to tell the time of day by the sun's shadow had fled in favor of more reliable methods. Here, a stone sundial with an ornamental metal gnomon is surrounded by flourishing pots of pelargoniums with their tall heads of blossom straining upward.*

Opposite page: *This spacious, tree-lined avenue bespeaks peace and tranquility; the trellis-backed seat at the far end offers a place for the walker to rest and enjoy the atmosphere offered by mature trees covered with and underplanted by English ivy. The shapes of the sparsely leafed branches create graceful patterns against the sky. The very simplicity of the design plays a large part in the harmonious feeling it evokes.*

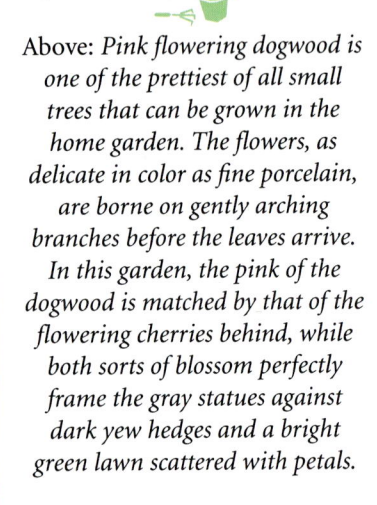

Above: *Pink flowering dogwood is one of the prettiest of all small trees that can be grown in the home garden. The flowers, as delicate in color as fine porcelain, are borne on gently arching branches before the leaves arrive. In this garden, the pink of the dogwood is matched by that of the flowering cherries behind, while both sorts of blossom perfectly frame the gray statues against dark yew hedges and a bright green lawn scattered with petals.*

Left: *A restful oasis is created in this cozy home garden with a graveled area flanked on all sides by flowers and foliage. Welcoming seating is provided by rustic twig chairs and settee and a weathered, carved wooden bench, centered around a small stone table, while potted ferns and begonias line up along the edges of the graveled area. The gnarled old tree in the background lends the character of its twisting branches to the scene.*

Left: *Pink-flowered varieties of the tulip or saucer magnolia frame a thick, sloping meadow laden with daffodils. Trumpet and large-cupped daffodils in yellow and white have been allowed to naturalize freely here to spectacular effect. To achieve these same naturalizing results, it is best to plant the daffodil bulbs fairly deeply and spaced well apart.*

Below: *"Borrowed landscape" is a term that originated in Japan, but it has been applied to gardens in many other parts of the world. Certainly this stunning Alaskan garden, which utilizes a spectacular view of mountains, inlet, and glacier as a backdrop, is a case in point. Allowing the garden to play off of the best natural features of the landscape (or even to hide the less attractive ones) is a principle that can be applied everywhere.*

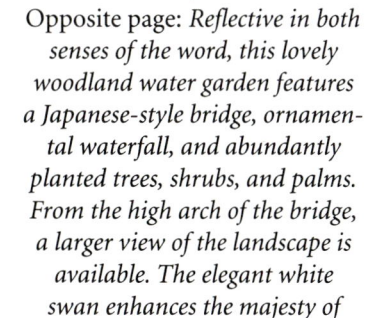

Opposite page: *Reflective in both senses of the word, this lovely woodland water garden features a Japanese-style bridge, ornamental waterfall, and abundantly planted trees, shrubs, and palms. From the high arch of the bridge, a larger view of the landscape is available. The elegant white swan enhances the majesty of this large-scale garden.*

ACHILLEA MILLEFOLIUM
YARROW
PERENNIAL; HARDY TO ZONE 2

The flat, platelike flower heads of yarrow bloom all summer in a choice range of colors including yellow, white, red, and pink. Its sturdy 2′ stems rarely need staking; this is an excellent perennial for cutting and for naturalizing in a sunny situation, such as a site along a fence.

AGERATUM HOUSTONIANUM
AGERATUM; FLOSS FLOWER
ANNUAL

This compact, bushy plant produces its distinctive, small, puffy flowers in bright or pastel shades of blue over somewhat hairy leaves from June to September. At about 6″ tall, it is a classic edging plant for a sunny border; it also makes a good potted plant.

AJUGA REPTANS
BUGLE; BUGLEWEED
PERENNIAL; HARDY TO ZONE 2

Ajuga can be invasive, but the variegated leaves and blue flower spikes of some selections make it an attractive ground cover for difficult areas such as bare spots under trees and shrubs. Ajuga prefers part sun to dappled shade and adequate moisture, but it is adaptable.

ANEMONE X HYBRIDA
JAPANESE ANEMONE
PERENNIAL; HARDY TO ZONE 5

Anemones grow best in a partly shaded locale with plenty of moisture but also with good drainage. The delicate flowers in pink, rose, or white—colors unusual for a fall bloomer like this—appear to float atop the 2–3′ tall stems.

ANTIRRHINUM MAJUS
SNAPDRAGON
PERENNIAL; HARDY TO ZONE 8

These country flowers are fondly remembered by all who used to "snap" the blooms in childhood. Varieties are available from 4″ (good for edging or in pots) to 2′ (good for mid-border) in a great many colors and color combinations. All types appreciate sun and water.

AQUILEGIA HYBRIDS
COLUMBINE
PERENNIAL; HARDY TO ZONE 3

Their finely divided foliage and dainty, nodding blooms make columbines a favorite wherever they are grown. Long-spurred hybrids come in several gorgeous bicolors. These plants like part shade to full sun and good drainage. They will self-sow but are not overly invasive.

CHRYSANTHEMUM PARTHENIUM
FEVERFEW
PERENNIAL; HARDY TO ZONE 4

This ancient garden herb was formerly used medicinally; now it is grown for its cheerful, button-shaped flowers. At around 12″ tall, it fits comfortably in pots or beds. A spot in full sun and with good drainage but ample watering will meet its needs.

CIMICIFUGA RACEMOSA
BUGBANE; BLACK SNAKEROOT
PERENNIAL; HARDY TO ZONE 4

The common names of this plant are in complete contradiction to the airy simplicity of its handsome 3′ tall wands of fluffy, white flowers. A good choice for naturalizing, these shade-loving perennials have attractively divided foliage and enjoy well-watered woodland conditions.

COREOPSIS LANCEOLATA
COREOPSIS; TICKSEED
PERENNIAL; HARDY TO ZONE 3

Golden-yellow coreopsis carries a profusion of 1″ flowers on bushy, 1–3′ tall plants with fine, delicate foliage. A good plant for the front of the border, coreopsis enjoys full sun and will grow vigorously in almost any well-drained soil.

DIANTHUS BARBATUS
SWEET WILLIAM
BIENNIAL; HARDY TO ZONE 3

The spicy-scented, zigzag-edged flowers in pink, red, and white are borne in clusters at the end of 18″ stems from May to July, with sometimes a second flush in fall. They enjoy a sunny site and do not mind dry soil.

ECHINACEA PURPUREA
CONEFLOWER
PERENNIAL; HARDY TO ZONE 3

Purple or white petals surround the cone-shaped centers of this perennial, which grows from 2–4′ tall and blooms from June through September. A classic plant for naturalizing, coneflower likes full sun and handles heat and dry conditions well.

EUPATORIUM PURPUREUM
JOE PYE WEED
PERENNIAL; HARDY TO ZONE 3

This spreading, occasionally invasive North American wildflower is best grown at the back of a border or naturalized in an open spot in full sun. The vanilla-scented, fluffy, pink flower heads on 3–5′ stems are classic mixers for informal country bouquets.

GAURA LINDHEIMERI
GAURA
PERENNIAL; HARDY TO ZONE 5

These graceful plants bear airy collections of dainty, white flowers that fade to pink. It blooms in May and again in fall, and will bloom intermittently during the summer if the initial spikes are removed after bloom. It prefers full sun and a dry, nonclay soil.

GERANIUM SANGUINEUM
BLOODY CRANESBILL
PERENNIAL; HARDY TO ZONE 4

The small but handsome red flowers of this hardy geranium appear from May to September over lobed leaves on 10″ stems. The foliage turns an attractive shade of red in the fall. This plant fits well at the front of the border with part sun to part shade.

HEMEROCALLIS HYBRIDS
DAYLILY
PERENNIAL; HARDY TO ZONE 3

These popular plants often grow along country lanes, where they have naturalized from gardens. A wonderful group for naturalizing or for borders, daylilies merit inclusion in any country garden. Many colors, heights, and bloom times are available. Most varieties prefer sun but will grow in partial shade.

HESPERIS MATRONALIS
SWEET ROCKET; DAME'S VIOLET
PERENNIAL; HARDY TO ZONE 4

Sweet rocket's umbels of white or pale lilac flowers on 3–4′ stalks flourish in part sun to shade from May to June. Though short-lived, the plants often self-sow, making them good candidates for naturalizing. The flowers are fragrant, and the scent is stronger at night.

IRIS SPECIES
BEARDED IRIS
PERENNIAL; HARDY TO ZONE 3

Nicknamed "The Rainbow Flower," tall bearded iris comes in a wider range of colors and patterns than almost any other blossom. At about 3′ tall, most varieties are good for the middle or back of the border or along a fence. They love full sun and shallow planting.

LATHYRUS LATIFOLIUS
EVERLASTING PEA; PERENNIAL PEA
PERENNIAL VINE; HARDY TO ZONE 4

This scentless but hardy relative of the annual sweet pea is excellent for covering a fence, shed, or tree stump. Pink or white blooms grace the 10′ vine from May to July, followed by seed pods that resemble edible snap peas. Full sun or part shade will suit this adaptable climber.

LILIUM TRUMPET HYBRIDS
TRUMPET LILIES; AURELIAN LILIES
BULB; HARDY TO ZONE 5

These fragrant lily varieties are available in rose, white, yellow, orange, and pink, some striped with darker color on the outside. Most have multiple 4–6″ long flowers on 4–7′ stems; many may need staking. A spot where the bulbs are shaded and the foliage is in sunlight is best.

LUPINUS POLYPHYLLUS HYBRIDS
LUPINES
BULB; HARDY TO ZONE 3

Generous spires of pea-type flowers in a multitude of colors rise over attractive foliage from May through July, depending on the variety. Dwarf cultivars are 10–12″ tall, while standard types can reach 3′. All lupines like moist soil and a cool spot in sun to part shade.

MYOSOTIS SYLVATICA
FORGET-ME-NOT
PERENNIAL; HARDY TO ZONE 3

Forget-me-nots have a compact habit that makes them good edging plants. They reseed readily and establish colonies that continue for years, doing their best in a moist soil in partial shade but blooming under a fairly wide range of conditions.

OENOTHERA FRUTICOSA
SUNDROPS
PERENNIAL; HARDY TO ZONE 4

These perennial, day-blooming relatives of the biennial evening primrose spread but are easily controlled. A good plant for the middle of the border, this North American native sports cheerful yellow flowers from June through September. A spot in full sun to part shade will suit it best.

PEROVSKIA ATRIPLICIFOLIA
RUSSIAN SAGE
PERENNIAL; HARDY TO ZONE 4

This shrublike perennial produces blue spikes of flowers on a 36″ tall plant with fine silver-tinted foliage, offering a nice misty color contribution to the back of the border. Full sun suits it best; the blooming season is from July through September.

PHYSOSTEGIA VIRGINIANA
OBEDIENT PLANT
PERENNIAL; HARDY TO ZONE 3

Attractive pink, rose, or lavender flowers bloom on 18–20″ stems from August through September. They will sit well in the middle of a border, but they spread quickly and need to be cut to the ground after blooming. Full sun is best, but the plants will tolerate some shade.

PLATYCODON GRANDIFLORUS
BALLOON FLOWER
PERENNIAL; HARDY TO ZONE 3

The large, showy blooms of this perennial range in color through blue, pink, violet, and white. Appearing in balloon-shaped buds, the flowers open into 2–3″ bell or saucer shapes. Platycodons are pretty, graceful, fairly tall country favorites for sun to part shade.

RUDBECKIA NITIDA
RUDBECKIA
PERENNIAL; HARDY TO ZONE 4

These relatives of the black-eyed susan may be grown in much the same way as their better-known cousins. Full sun and good drainage suit these 3–5′ plants, which bloom from July to September. The golden-petaled flowers with dark, raised centers are very good for cutting.

SENECIO CINERARIA
DUSTY MILLER
TENDER PERENNIAL; HARDY TO ZONE 8

Grown for its beautifully cut silvery leaves rather than for its plain yellow flowers, dusty miller is a classic edging plant that is also good for containers. It combines wonderfully well with pink geraniums, both for color and because both enjoy sun and good drainage.

TULIPA DARWIN HYBRIDS
TULIPS
BULB; HARDY TO ZONE 3

These are the classic, strong-stemmed tulips with large single blooms that have been grown in country gardens for generations. Blooming time is in April or May; these are excellent, strong-stemmed flowers for cutting.

VERBENA SPECIES
VERVAIN
PERENNIAL; HARDY TO ZONE 4

The relaxed, trailing growth habit of these summer-blooming plants makes them wonderful choices for softening the lines of pots and window boxes. Most have small, oval, serrated leaves along long stems that produce rounded heads of brightly colored flowers. They need sun, water, and well-drained soil.

VERONICA LONGIFOLIA
VERONICA; SPEEDWELL
PERENNIAL; HARDY TO ZONE 4

Versatile veronica performs well in many different situations: as a ground cover, a border plant, or even in the rock garden. This perennial of spreading habit is not fussy regarding soil type or situation, though it prefers a site with some sun.

VINCA MINOR
CREEPING MYRTLE; LESSER PERIWINKLE
PERENNIAL; HARDY TO ZONE 4

This creeping evergreen vine is one of the best ground-cover plants for shaded areas. Pretty blue pinwheel flowers dot the glossy, dark green foliage in May; sometimes the plant will rebloom in fall. You can interplant this ground cover with spring bulbs.

VIOLA X WITTROCKIANA
PANSY
ANNUAL

The central dark blotches characteristic of many cultivars give the flowers the appearance of having tiny catlike faces. A longtime country favorite, pansies are good in pots, at the front of the border, lining a walkway, and for cutting. They like some shade and a moist soil.

Natural Gardens

From the desert Southwest to the vast Great Plains, from the hot summers and below-freezing winters of the north to the salt spray of the maritime east and the mild and rainy northwest coast—the North American continent contains an almost dizzying variety of climates and environments. With this superabundance of natural environments comes also a wonderful variety of beautiful and interesting native plant life.

It makes gardening easier and pays homage to an area's horticultural heritage to include some plants that are native to your area, or that may hail from elsewhere in the world but thrive under similar conditions. Xeriscaping, especially useful in arid areas that are naturally hot and dry, replaces the large expanses of lawn and thirsty garden flowers with landscaped areas of striking cacti and desert plants. This saves on water in areas subject to drought and creates a garden area that functions as a more natural part of its environment.

Right: *This drought-resistant planting uses bright yellow daisies, artemisia, sea lavender, and woody Japanese black pines to create a memorable strolling garden that is naturally suited to its environment.* Above: Eschscholzia californica.

Right: *The desert terrain of the southwestern United States plays host to some wonderfully interesting and attractive flora. These make exciting landscaping subjects, and since they are preadapted to the arid climate, they require no elaborate irrigation schemes to ensure their survival. The brilliant cerise-colored* Penstemon parryii *and the scarlet flowers of* Justicia spicigera *here combine to form a handsome and drought-resistant ground cover that will bloom all summer.*

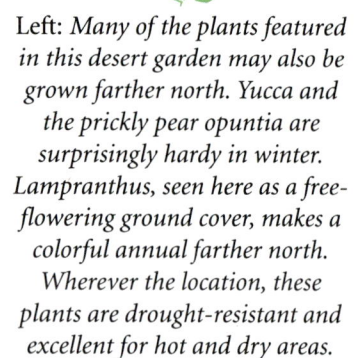

Left: *Many of the plants featured in this desert garden may also be grown farther north. Yucca and the prickly pear opuntia are surprisingly hardy in winter. Lampranthus, seen here as a free-flowering ground cover, makes a colorful annual farther north. Wherever the location, these plants are drought-resistant and excellent for hot and dry areas.*

Left: A collector's dream of cacti dominates the foreground of this sunny, warm-weather yard. In contrast, the space in the background is laid out as a conventional grassy lawn, just large enough to accommodate outdoor recreation. Maintaining a lawn in the desert requires careful watering, while using cacti such as the golden barrel and organ-pipe cactus shown here creates a handsome setting that is water conservative and nearly trouble free.

Opposite page: *Caught as it is between the desert and the seacoast, beautiful Southern California contains a multitude of microclimates and allows for many different styles of planting. This brightly blooming site overlooking the ocean has a Mediterranean feel and utilizes species that love a sandy, sunny location and do not mind mist or salt spray. Almost no extra watering is required to maintain the beauty of* Echium fastuosum, *tree lupine, and gazania.*

Above: *Almost any garden plant will adapt well to a situation similar to that favored by its wild species ancestors. In this California garden, cultivated varieties of native plants thrive in a setting similar to the rocky scrub occurring in their natural habitats. Succulents such as agave and yucca mix well with the silver, shrubby cushion bush,* Nemesia capensis, *and* Penstemon 'Skyline.'

Right: *Not all cacti are desert dwellers; this striking collection unexpectedly combines the elongated, ropelike forms of a jungle cactus with the more familiar round globes of the desert-adapted golden barrel cactus. A site with good drainage in the mild climate of Southern California pleases both types. Both selections blossom, jungle cactus producing large, scented flowers, and golden barrel displaying springtime crowns of smaller blooms.*

Right: *Some of the most versatile of all garden perennials were bred from ultra-hardy meadow and prairie plants from the Great Plains of the United States. These habitats, though often appearing somewhat flat and featureless topographically, were teeming microcosms supporting a vast range of wildlife. Plants such as these aster, purple coneflower, rudbeckia, and liatris share the traits of hardiness, disease resistance, and a long season of bloom.*

Right: *Summer-blooming prairie perennials are adaptable to a wide range of growing conditions; here they are protected from extreme heat by being grown in partial shade.* Achillea ptarmica 'The Pearl' *is a white-flowered cousin of the more frequently grown yellow yarrow, and the red-and-yellow columbine seen here,* Aquilegia canadensis, *is a wild relative of the large, long-spurred garden hybrid columbines.*

Opposite page: *Two of the most beautiful and beloved of all Western wildflowers, pink evening primrose and Texas bluebonnet, are naturalized together in this meadow planting at the edge of a stand of small trees. These plants will create similar swathes of color anywhere they are allowed to, but they also may be easily kept under control by dividing the clumps every few years.*

Right: *The term "xeriscaping" is gaining wide use as more gardeners discover that water-saving gardening makes good environmental sense and saves time, energy, and effort—commodities that all gardeners occasionally have in short supply. Even plots in the relatively rainy northeast benefit from the inclusion of such perennials as Russian sage (perovskia),* Sedum *'Autumn Joy,' and* Rudbeckia fulgida, *and ornamental grasses such as pennisetum and eragrostis, which are both beautiful and drought resistant.*

Left: *A wide variety of plants lend themselves to water-conserving gardening, as illustrated by this imaginative combination of cacti, conifers, and grasses. Exhibiting a wonderful crop of its edible fruits, which will soon redden, a hardy prickly pear grows happily alongside the blue and gold cultivars of the evergreen* Chamaecyparis pisifera. *The drought-resistant ornamental grass* Miscanthus sinensis *'Variegatus' creates a fountainlike effect (without the use of water) in the background.*

Left: *Choosing plants with care can add greatly to the ease with which a garden can be cared for. Perennials such as those shown here are good choices; positioning them close together so that the plants shade each others' roots and keep the soil cool means that they will require watering less frequently even though they are planted in a fairly sunny spot.*

Artemisia tridentata
Sage Brush
Shrub; hardy to zone 7

This 5′ tall, silvery shrub is a familiar sight in the American West and Southwest. Its lax shape makes it a good candidate for a naturally landscaped area rather than for formal clipping. The aromatic, toothed foliage and peeling bark add to its textured charm.

Aster alpinus
Rock Aster
Perennial; hardy to zone 3

Unlike most of its fall-blooming relatives, the compact rock aster sprouts its purple or white flowers in spring and summer. Growing in small, spreading tufts, it makes a bright ground cover and will do well in any sunny location that has well-drained soil.

Callirhoe involucrata
Wine Cups; Poppy Mallows
Perennial; hardy to zone 4

The long taproot of this drought-resistant plant allows it to glean water from deep below the soil's surface. It is an excellent choice for dry, sunny slopes or banks, where the cupped, satiny, plum-colored flowers and floppy foliage would make a wonderful summer show.

Crambe maritima
Sea Kale
Perennial; hardy to zone 4

The large, lobed, blue-green leaves of this plant make a strong presence in a wild garden. Cultivated as a vegetable 400 years ago in Europe, it tolerates salt well and so is prized in coastal areas. Small, fragrant, white flowers bloom in summer.

Eschscholzia californica
California Poppy
Annual

Easy to grow, this golden wildflower thrives in dry, sunny areas, even in poor soil, and will self-sow freely when conditions suit it. Hybrids are available in yellow, pink, orange, white, and cream, as well as the original gold.

Euryops species
Perennial; hardy to zone 5

This small, shrublike perennial has gray stems and silvery, needlelike leaves on a neat, mounded plant that makes a smart accent to a natural-style landscape. Small, yellow daisy-like flowers appear in summer for an interesting contrast to the foliage. This plant likes sun and dislikes damp soil.

Oenothera caespitosa
Perennial; hardy to zone 6

This low-growing member of the evening primrose family has white flowers that open their four heart-shaped petals at dusk on summer evenings. Dainty in looks and character, it needs a light, dry soil and protection from too much winter moisture.

Opuntia basilaris
Prickly Pear
Cactus; hardy to zone 6

The prickly pear can be quite hardy and makes an unexpected addition to cold-weather areas; when combined with yucca, it can bring a feeling of the Old West. It does not flower readily, but its unusual shape and colorful spines are attractive in their own right.

PANICUM VIRGATUM
SWITCH GRASS
PERENNIAL; HARDY TO ZONE 3

The 3′ tall, fountainlike leaves of this ornamental grass are topped by feathery inflorescences in summer to fall. The leaves turn red or yellow (depending upon the variety) in fall and make an especially nice note of color in the autumn mixed border. Any soil will do.

PENSTEMON COBAEA
PENSTEMON
PERENNIAL; HARDY TO ZONE 5

The tubular, white-flushed lilac flowers of this perennial bloom on 2′ stalks over the plant's pointed, green leaves all summer long. An excellent choice for a sunny spot, this plant divides well, but it is tall and may require staking.

PENSTEMON PARRYII
PENSTEMON; BEARDTONGUE
PERENNIAL; HARDY TO ZONE 7

Showy, tubular blooms and an adaptable, trouble-free nature make penstemons worthy of a place in any sunny garden spot. Flowers come in colors including red, pink, yellow, blue, and white; the red shades are attractive to hummingbirds.

SALVIA GREGII
AUTUMN SAGE
PERENNIAL; HARDY TO ZONE 8

The tubular flowers of this Texas native are bright carmine red and appear from midsummer to fall. Though not hardy in colder areas, it may be grown there as an annual. It makes a nice dash of color for a sunny corner or the base of a south-facing wall.

SEDUM SPECTABILE
SEDUM
PERENNIAL; HARDY TO ZONE 4

This versatile species and its cultivars constitute a mainstay of the late summer and autumn garden. Flat flower heads in shades of red and rose bloom in any situation over gray-green, succulent foliage; the dried flower heads continue to look attractive in the winter garden.

SILPHIUM TEREBENTHINACEUM
PRAIRIE DOCK
PERENNIAL; HARDY TO ZONE 4

Clusters of flowers top a tall, naked stalk that may reach 9′ in summer. The huge, heart-shaped leaves look almost tropical. Excellent in a natural meadow or prairie planting, the plant does best in sun to part shade with a moist but well-drained soil.

THERMOPSIS MONTANA
FALSE LUPINE
PERENNIAL; HARDY TO ZONE 4

The light yellow flower spires of these lupine look-alikes bloom in early and midsummer. They can be distinguished from true lupines by the wider leaves, divided into threes. Easily grown, they make an excellent addition to the wild garden, where they will have room to spread and increase.

YUCCA GLAUCA
YUCCA
PERENNIAL; HARDY TO ZONE 3

The architectural quality of the yucca is practically without equal among hardy plants. Surprisingly hardy, it lends a touch of the Mediterranean or the desert to cool-weather gardens. Its compact spire of flowers appears in summer.

Foliage Gardens

Though greenery is relegated to the chorus in many gardens while blossoms play the starring role, foliage can still be an important component of any garden design. The delicately divided leaves of ferns and the fountainlike effects offered by many ornamental grasses have a beauty and grace all their own. Such foliage not only serves as a lovely background to blooms but can often be used as the dominant feature of a garden design. Foliage also carries a garden through the seasons, long after the flowers have faded to a memory.

Far from being simply green, some foliage plants offer variegated patterns of white, gold, and red, while others have leaves tinged with yellow, blue, or bronze that can act as a focal point or an accent in a color scheme. Tall, flowing grasses and dense, leafy ferns are ideal for creating a lush and generous look in a small patch of earth. A variety of foliage plants also do well in shady, moist areas that most floral plants find to be withering.

Right: *Colorful crotons* (Codiaeum variegatum) *cover the middle ground in this Florida garden, while liriope provide an edging and lady palms serve as a rich green background.* Above: Neoregelia carolinea.

Right: *The popularity of hostas as landscape plants has taken off in recent years, and deservedly so. These handsome perennials are practically trouble free and are excellent choices for filling shaded locations. A double helping of a white-margined cultivar here anchors a green-and-white border that also includes ferns, foam-flower, and bleeding heart.*

Left: *Two very different hosta cultivars, one with narrow, variegated leaves showing undulated margins and the other with large, pleated, blue-green leaves in classic "plantain lily" style, demonstrate the different effects breeders have achieved with these plants. The contrast between the two makes a wonderful garden combination and acts as a foil for the rhododendron and evergreen behind. These are not in bloom, but most hostas also bear attractive, often sweetly fragrant lily-shaped flowers in shades of white and lavender during summertime.*

Left: *Their almost infinite variability of leaf color, texture, size, and form means that hostas can carry a planting scheme all by themselves; all sorts of them will combine well with each other. Some varieties make ever-larger foliage rosettes with age, while others spread to form new clumps. Here,* Saxifraga stolonifera *and* Begonia grandis *add further to the foliar display.*

Opposite page: *The Victorians had a passion for growing ferns in gardens and for pressing their leaves between the pages of plant-collecting albums; the lacy, finely cut leaves, found in many different shapes and shades of green, inspired this affection. Plants such as these ostrich ferns and wood ferns will thrive in a well-drained woodland setting like the glen shown here.*

Right: *As beautiful and eye-catching as a piece of sculpture, the cinnamon-dusted fiddleheads of new fern fronds stretch open to show ever-more fresh green. The shape and location of this specimen make it a focal point; the placement is very carefully chosen, as the warm fern color stands out against the gray rocks and path, and the contrast of the English bluebells makes a beautiful backdrop.*

Above: *Though a mixture of fern species always creates a strong effect, a large stand dominated by a single species can also be a standout. Here, masses of ostrich fern accented with a few hay-scented ferns create a wonderfully feathery feel, quite different in texture from a combination of many different varieties but no less attractive. The spotted leaves of lungwort peep through in the foreground, and blue campanulas rise behind.*

Opposite page: *Ornamental grasses have found a place in many home gardens, partly as a result of the "New American Garden" movement in the 1980s. Their attraction lies in form and pattern, and when allowed the space to show off their almost sculptural habits of growth, they are superb performers.* Miscanthus transmorrisonensis, *shown here, prefers a damp soil and so is an excellent choice for planting near water. Its size also makes it valuable for use as a windbreak.*

Above: *The plumes of ornamental grasses can be even showier than their fountainlike foliage, and the great height of the plants allows them to work as a strong center-piece to a planting. The silvery-pink plumes of* Pennisetum setaceum *make lovely specimens; this one is given added emphasis by the pink and red annuals (nicotiana and zinnia) planted around it.*

Left: *A selection of different perennial grasses makes an attractive and nearly mainte-nance-free summer grouping around this small patio. The loosely kept plants offer the added benefit of screening the chaise lounges to create a place for solitude and relaxation.*

Right: *The heart-shaped leaves of the elephant's ear plant (Coloca- sia esculenta) make a bold impact in the tropical garden, somewhat similar to the effect of large-leaved hostas in temperate locations. Here, they are partnered with scarlet cannas and dwarf banana. Gardeners in cooler locations can enjoy tropical plants such as these by growing tender plants in pots, moving them outdoors for sum- mer, and taking them back indoors for the winter.*

Right: *This intriguing mix of temperate and tropical species also features colocasia but adds two forms of pennisetum and the unexpected addition of statuesque Zea mays—corn. Technically classed as annual grasses, corn plants bear tassels that are decid- edly decorative. Using vegetables as ornamentals within the garden can create some inspired pairings, and such companion planting also often has the benefit of discouraging insect pests.*

Opposite page: *A thriving collec- tion of bromeliads have colonized the branches of a tree as well as the ground and rocks beneath. Bromeliads are epiphytes, which derive most of their nutrition from rainfall and decaying leaf material. Roots cling to the branches, but the plants are not parasitic and do not harm the supporting trees. Bromeliads such as neoregelia are greenhouse subjects in temperate regions but will grow outdoors in warm areas.*

HOSTA DECORATA
PERENNIAL; HARDY TO ZONE 3

This hosta species, with its attractive, wide, white-rimmed leaves, is a good choice for shade or woodland gardens, as it likes a moist, sandy soil in a place out of the sun. Numerous lilac, trumpet-shaped flowers appear in panicles in midsummer, and it spreads to form a ground cover.

HOSTA FORTUNEI
PERENNIAL; HARDY TO ZONE 3

Many of the hostas in this group have attractively variegated leaves; examples include 'Albopicta' and 'Aurea-Marginata.' Pale violet flowers add a nice touch to the picture, making these wonderful accents for shade.

HOSTA 'FRANCEE'
PERENNIAL; HARDY TO ZONE 3

The large, heart-shaped leaves of this cultivar of *Hosta fortunei* are elegantly edged with creamy white. Spikes of lavender, trumpet-shaped flowers appear in summer, enhancing the show. 'Francee' does well in shady spots and grows rapidly, eventually reaching a substantial size.

HOSTA HYBRIDS
PERENNIAL; HARDY TO ZONE 3

Abundant hybrid choices are now available, as the popularity of this versatile perennial continues to increase. Plants are available with small and narrow to large and broad leaves, which may include the colors blue and gold, and may have white or cream splashes or edges.

HOSTA SIEBOLDIANA
PERENNIAL; HARDY TO ZONE 3

The large, puckered, blue-gray leaves of this hosta are beautiful as a ground cover for shade, but they may turn dull green in the sun. Lilac flowers appear above the heart-shaped foliage in early summer.

HOSTA SIEBOLDII
PERENNIAL; HARDY TO ZONE 3

Also known as *H. albomarginata*, this plant has narrow, lance-shaped leaves with handsome, irregular edges. Violet flowers are followed by green seed pods that turn brown and can be used effectively in floral arrangements.

HOSTA TARDIFLORA
PERENNIAL; HARDY TO ZONE 3

This hosta is somewhat slower-growing than some others but eventually forms sizable clumps. Its arrow-shaped, dark green leaves have a thick texture, and the large racemes of pale purple flowers appear in autumn just above the leaves. This compact plant is good where space is limited.

HOSTA VENTRICOSA
PERENNIAL; HARDY TO ZONE 3

This species, unlike some others, usually comes true from seed. The glossy, heart-shaped leaves have attractive wavy margins. Like other hostas, it is excellent for landscaping by a pool. Variegated forms exist.

ADIANTUM PEDATUM
NORTHERN MAIDENHAIR FERN;
FIVE-FINGER FERN
DECIDUOUS FERN; HARDY TO ZONE 3

The narrow, medium-green fronds of this fern are delicately divided along glossy, dark brown to black stems, making this a pretty and graceful plant that requires a moist, shady spot. A dwarf relative, *A. aleuticum* var. *subpumilum*, tolerates some sun.

ATHYRIUM NIPONICUM 'PICTUM'
JAPANESE PAINTED FERN
DECIDUOUS FERN; HARDY TO ZONE 3

This very attractive small fern shows up very well near steps or at the base of a tree and has a very decorative effect in a partly shady spot. Stems are reddish-purple and fronds are green-brushed silver, sometimes with a slight flush of purple on the reverse.

BLECHNUM SPICANT
HARD FERN; DEER FERN
EVERGREEN FERN; HARDY TO ZONE 4

This fern has narrowly divided leathery fronds and tolerates dry conditions better than some other ferns, making it fairly easy to cultivate. It does appreciate some humus added to the soil, and it dislikes lime.

DRYOPTERIS AFFINIS
GOLDEN SCALED MALE FERN
EVERGREEN FERN; HARDY TO ZONE 4

The large, rich green fronds of this fern grow upright in a graceful, arching shape. The plant can grow to be 4' tall, making it a good landscaping item. Golden scales cover the stems and give this fern its common name.

DRYOPTERIS FELIX-MAS
MALE FERN
DECIDUOUS FERN; HARDY TO ZONE 4

Its tolerance for sun and dry soil and its propensity for self-sowing make this *Dryopteris* a favorite for ground cover and for naturalizing. Its large, arching fronds that typify the fern family make it very attractive.

MATTEUCIA STRUTHIOPTERIS
OSTRICH FERN
DECIDUOUS FERN; HARDY TO ZONE 2

Large fronds reminiscent of ostrich plumes give this fern its characteristic look. It grows in the shape of a vase or shuttle-cock and spreads by underground runners, making it good for naturalizing. Easy to grow, it prefers moist shade but will tolerate a variety of conditions.

OSMUNDA REGALIS
ROYAL FERN
DECIDUOUS FERN; HARDY TO ZONE 3

This tall, upright fern sprouts long, elegantly divided fronds that are somewhat oval in outline as it grows. It requires acidic soil and prefers shade but will grow in some sun. When young, its fronds have a subtle pinkish cast.

POLYSTICHUM SETIFERUM
SOFT SHIELD FERN; HEDGE FERN
EVERGREEN FERN; HARDY TO ZONE 5

This fern is one without a strong preference for wet over dry conditions, making it a versatile choice. With an arching shape and fronds so intricately divided that they have a mosslike or filigreed appearance, it serves as a good contrast plant for more robust ferns.

CALAMAGROSTIS ACUTIFLORA
REED GRASS
PERENNIAL; HARDY TO ZONE 4

Golden, fan-shaped plumes on tall stalks combine with the light green foliage of this clump-forming grass to make a striking picture. It does best in sun but will tolerate some shade. Unusual variegated forms are available.

CHASMANTHEUM LATIFOLIUM
NORTHERN SEA OATS
PERENNIAL; HARDY TO ZONE 5

The bright green, pointed leaves of this 3′ tall grass sprout from slender, upright stems in a way reminiscent of bamboo. Partial shade is best for this plant, which forms decorative clumps and bears attractive flattened seed heads from late summer through fall.

DESCHAMPSIA CAESPITOSA
TUFTED HAIRGRASS
PERENNIAL; HARDY TO ZONE 3

The dark foliage of this grass remains green all year long, creating a point of winter interest in the border. Small, brown flower spikes are produced in summer but last into the winter. Sun or shade is suitable.

HELICTOTRICHON SEMPERVIRENS
AVENA GRASS; BLUE OAT GRASS
PERENNIAL; HARDY TO ZONE 4

Blue oat grass produces light yellow flower spikes in the summer and stiff spikes of silvery-blue leaves, giving the plant a distinctive color effect. This interesting plant makes a fine structural accent and will thrive in a dry, sunny area.

MISCANTHUS SINENSIS
MAIDEN GRASS
PERENNIAL; HARDY TO ZONE 5

The very narrow, ribbed leaves of this grass arch gracefully when young and sometimes curl into spirals when dry. A yellow-striped form is known as 'Zebrinus' or Zebra grass. This grass has a very refined, dainty appearance and likes a sunny, dry situation.

PENNISETUM ALOPECUROIDES
CHINESE FOUNTAIN GRASS
PERENNIAL; HARDY TO ZONE 5

This fountain grass creates an attractive picture in late summer and fall when its stems, topped by cylindrical, purple-tinged bristles, arch over the deep green foliage. This handsome grass requires dry soil and the warmth of the full sun.

PENNISETUM SETACEUM
AFRICAN FOUNTAIN GRASS
PERENNIAL; HARDY TO ZONE 8

Less hardy than many other grasses, this species will still tolerate a bit of frost but not a hard freeze. Spiked, rose-pink panicles appear over the arching foliage in summer and last well into winter.

SPODIOPOGON SIBERICUS
FROST GRASS
PERENNIAL; HARDY TO ZONE 4

This grass makes an outstanding accent for the foliage garden, especially in the fall, when the silver flower heads fade and the broad leaves turn a lovely deep golden shade. This sun-lover grows 3–5′ tall and makes a wonderful specimen.

CANNA X GENERALIS
CANNA
RHIZOME; HARDY TO ZONE 7

Though not hardy, this plant does well in summer beddings. Dwarf varieties succeed in pots, while the standard size is good for the back of a border. Its large spikes of flowers in the brighter tones of yellow, pink, red, and orange and its handsome, broad foliage make it a favorite.

CODIAEUM VARIEGATUM
CROTON
SHRUB; HARDY TO ZONE 10

This shrub offers foliage in technicolor combinations of pink, red, cream, orange, green, yellow, and black. It's an excellent potted plant for cold climates, but it does not survive outdoor temperatures below about 50°F.

COLOCASIA ESCULENTA
ELEPHANT'S EAR; TARO ROOT
TUBER; HARDY TO ZONE 9

A luxuriously tropical effect can be created with the enormous heart-shaped leaves of colocasia. The foliage may have prominent white veins, which add to the plant's beauty. It is evergreen in warm areas and likes to be planted near water; it may be grown in a large container.

HEDYCHIUM GARDNERIANUM
YELLOW GINGER LILY
PERENNIAL; HARDY TO ZONE 9

This large, upright tropical produces lance-shaped green leaves, crowned with scented spikes of light yellow and red flowers in late summer to autumn. Yellow ginger lily enjoys a moist soil and full sun, and is a good candidate for container planting.

MUSA SPECIES
BANANAS
PERENNIAL; HARDY TO ZONE 10

Though they resemble palm trees, bananas are neither trees nor palms, but large-statured perennials. The large, light green leaves look as well when grown in a tub as when planted in the ground in warm areas.

NEOREGELIA SPECIES
BROMELIADS
PERENNIAL; HARDY TO ZONE 10

In warm climates, where they may be grown outside, these epiphytes make a magnificent display when encouraged to grow on a tree. Elsewhere, they make good house or greenhouse plants that bring a touch of the tropics to the garden when summered outdoors.

RICINIS COMMUNIS
CASTOR BEAN; CASTOR-OIL PLANT
TENDER SHRUB; HARDY TO ZONE 10

The large, star-shaped, deeply lobed leaves of this tender shrub command attention wherever it is planted. A red-leaved form of this poisonous plant also exists. A sunny position and plenty of room are both essential to its success.

VRIESIA SPECIES
BROMELIADS
PERENNIAL; HARDY TO ZONE 10

Many bromeliads are grown for their attractive, bright flower spikes as well as for their ornamental leaves. Some, like vriesia, can be watered by filling the central cup within the rosette of leaves. They may be grown under glass with culture similar to that of tropical orchids.

Fragrant Gardens

For many plant lovers, scent plays an important role in enjoying a garden. Fragrance adds an ineffable, almost magical quality to a planting scheme, enhancing the beauty of the flowers by the addition of pleasantly scented breezes wafting from the direction of the garden. Scented flowers thus are able to simultaneously appeal to two of our senses, instead of just one. Fragrance has a wonderful ability to trigger memory, as well—so often the flower fragrances that most appeal to us are the ones that we loved as children.

Leaves can be scented as well as flowers, as any lover of herbs may attest. The fragrances of lavender and of sweetbriar roses rise from the leaves as well as the flowers, and plants such as mints and scented geraniums are often grown for the pleasant smell their leaves produce when rubbed. Many plants keep their scent well enough to be dried and used in the making of potpourri—a way of keeping the reminder of one's garden around through the entire year.

Right: *This garden includes plants with aromatic foliage as well as those with scented blossoms. The fragrance of the roses freely wafts from the flowers, while the thyme and mint emit scent only when rubbed, making a walk around the plants a pleasant treat.* Above: Rosa *'Peace.'*

Opposite page: *This romantically designed garden setting features sweetly scented flowers, both tender and hardy. One of the most fragrant and loved of all, the rose, appears prominently in shades of pink, red, and white. Modern hybrid tea roses have brighter colors and a longer season of bloom, but old roses have no equals for fragrance. Citrus trees, represented here by a pair of standard lemons, have aromatic flowers as well as fruit and may be pot-grown in the north.*

Above: *Not all peonies are fragrant, but the 'Bowl of Beauty' variety shown here is quite so. Its enormous pink-and-yellow flowers make a splashy show next to two other plants with scented blooms, Rosa 'Rita' and Dianthus 'Zing Rose.' This garden could also produce armfuls of scented bouquets, as all three of these flowers are excellent for cutting.*

Left: *The perfume from a large mixed border such as this can be heaven on a warm summer day, when the heat brings out delicious fragrances from both leaf and petal. This border includes* Phlox paniculata *'Bright Eyes,' purple-leaved* Perilla fruticosa, *and the white, lily-scented trumpets of* Hosta *'Royal Standard.'*

Opposite page: *The spectacular flowers of* Brugmansia suaveolens *give the plant its common name of angel's trumpet. The blooms also have a wonderful fragrance, which is especially pronounced at night; like many night-scented plants, its blossoms are pale in color. These large and beautiful plants can be grown as patio, house, or greenhouse subjects in cool areas, as they require winter protection. They are poisonous, so grow them out of the reach of pets and children.*

Right: *The white flowers of tall* Nicotiana sylvestris *have aptly been compared to bursts of fireworks. Like the fireworks they resemble, they really come into their own at dusk, standing out in the border and sharing their perfume more freely after dark. Here they are accompanied by other fragrant plants, including their smaller relatives N. alata, petunias, and pungent but pleasant marigolds.*

Above: *The unmistakable fragrance of jasmine is legendary. Many species and varieties are available; all make excellent garden subjects in the south and marvelous potted plants in the north, although when potted they tend to stay smaller than those garden-grown and will never equal the spectacular display put on by this specimen of* Jasminum polyanthum. *The white flowers are pink or red in bud; their pale color coupled with a delicious fragrance surely makes this trellis-lined path a lovely place for moonlit strolls.*

Right: *Some scented geraniums have attractive flowers in addition to their scented foliage. A broad range of leaf shapes and scents is available, and a collection of these plants (tender pot plants in cold-winter areas) makes a lovely, varied, and fragrant picture. Here, the large velvety leaves of peppermint-scented* Pelargonium tomentosum *mingle with rose-scented, lavender-bloomed P.* capitatum *to bedeck a white picket fence.*

Right: *Variegated and purple-leaved forms of familiar herbs are interplanted with the more common green-leaved varieties in this small herb garden, which offers delights for the eye, nose, and palate. Marjoram, mint, tarragon, sage, thyme, and basil are all prized both for scent and for culinary purposes. For gardeners with limited space, they can be made to flourish in containers such as this simple clay pot.*

Opposite page: *Many herbs are renowned for the scent of their leaves; those that retain their fragrance when dried are often used in making potpourris. This classically designed herb garden has been laid out to exhibit each plant to its best advantage so that a visitor could wander along the brick paths and stoop to sample the herbal aromas, including sage, lavender, thyme, and even the slightly bitter wormwood, which was valued in times past as a moth repellent.*

BRUGMANSIA SUAVEOLENS
ANGEL'S TRUMPET
SHRUB; HARDY TO ZONE 10

The spectacular dangling flowers of this tender shrub are shaped like large trumpets and are pleasantly fragrant, especially in the evening. Flowers come in pink, peach, yellow, orange, and white, but both seed and flowers are quite poisonous. It makes a good tub specimen.

CALAMINTHA NEPETOIDES
CALAMINT
PERENNIAL HERB; HARDY TO ZONE 4

This low-growing member of the mint family has pleasant mint-scented leaves, and its tiny but profuse white or pale lilac flowers appear in late summer to fall. Although small in stature, it will spread; it loves a sunny spot and will draw the attention of the local bee population.

HOSTA PLANTAGINEA
FRAGRANT HOSTA
PERENNIAL; HARDY TO ZONE 3

This hosta enjoys sunny conditions, though it will do well in partial shade. Leaves are oval, light green, and glossy, with prominent ribbing, but the real sources of delight are the sweetly fragrant flowers. The white, trumpet-shaped blooms open at dusk in late summer to fall.

JASMINUM POLYANTHUM
WINTER JASMINE
PERENNIAL VINE; HARDY TO ZONE 9

The lusciously scented, starry white flowers of this jasmine open in late winter to early spring. It makes a 10′ vine in warmer climates and may be grown in a greenhouse in temperate areas. Full sun and temperatures of 50–60°F in winter induce the most prolific bloom.

LAVANDULA ANGUSTIFOLIA
ENGLISH LAVENDER
PERENNIAL HERB; HARDY TO ZONE 5

This small shrub is often treated as a woody-stemmed perennial in the cooler part of its hardiness range. The purple spikes of flowers retain their clean scent even when dry; the silvery, needlelike leaves are also very aromatic. Full sun will encourage bloom production.

LILIUM 'CASA BLANCA'
ORIENTAL HYBRID LILY
BULB; HARDY TO ZONE 4

Lush blooms with a spicy scent are the hallmark of Oriental hybrid lilies, and the white, 8″ blooms of 'Casa Blanca' are no exception. At 4–6′ tall, it is a plant for the back of the garden, where it often needs staking. July and August are the peak of the blooming season.

MENTHA SPICATA
SPEARMINT
PERENNIAL HERB; HARDY TO ZONE 4

The toothed, rich green leaves of this perennial give off a wonderful aroma when rubbed and make a useful culinary herb. Though not a very large plant, it should be grown where the roots can be contained, as they spread rapidly. It prefers sun but will tolerate shade.

NICOTIANA SYLVESTRIS
NICOTIANA; FLOWERING TOBACCO
PERENNIAL; HARDY TO ZONE 9

This species of nicotiana carries tall panicles of fragrant, drooping, white flowers on 5′ stems in late summer, which have an especially spectacular appearance at dusk. A good choice for the evening-fragrant garden, it is often grown as an annual in temperate areas.

Paeonia lactiflora hybrids
PEONY
PERENNIAL; HARDY TO ZONE 3

P. lactiflora has produced many beautiful hybrids, including 'Albert Crousse,' 'Festiva Maxima,' and 'Sarah Bernhardt.' All bear large pink, red, or white flowers over attractively divided foliage in May or June. Peonies like sun and dislike root disturbance once planted.

Pelargonium graveolens
ROSE GERANIUM
PERENNIAL; HARDY TO ZONE 9

Scented geraniums can be grown as annuals or taken indoors for winter in areas where they are not hardy. They will grow in pots, hanging baskets, or as bedding plants. Scents range through floral, fruits, and spices; a collection of several varieties provides rare olfactory treats.

Perilla frutescens 'Atropurpurea'
PERILLA
ANNUAL

This unusual annual is grown primarily for its attractive, red-purple leaves, which release a pleasant scent when handled. The plant can be grown from seed and pinched to promote bushiness. It does well in a pot or as a summer bedding plant.

Phlox paniculata hybrids
PHLOX
PERENNIAL; HARDY TO ZONE 3

Its height and upright habit make this a favored plant for the back of the border. Hybrids come in shades of pink, red, and white, including bicolors; many have a pleasant scent. White-flowered varieties are especially good for the evening garden, as they show up well at dusk.

Rosa hybrid teas
ROSE
SHRUB; HARDY TO ZONE 4
WITH PROTECTION

Many modern rose hybrids fall into the hybrid tea category; these long-stemmed roses make wonderful garden plants for a well-drained, sunny spot, though they like ample watering. Their unmistakable scent makes them a popular feature of many fragrance gardens.

Salvia officinalis
SAGE
PERENNIAL HERB; HARDY TO ZONE 4
WITH PROTECTION

Sage's scented foliage, which can be used for cooking, also makes it an excellent choice for the fragrance garden. It grows well in either pot or border in a sunny situation but may succumb to very cold winters. A purple-leaved and tricolor form are also available.

Santolina chamaecyparissus
LAVENDER COTTON; SANTOLINA
PERENNIAL; HARDY TO ZONE 6

Tiny, needlelike leaves heavily covered with silvery-white felt make this a popular choice for its looks alone. Bright yellow, buttonlike flowers crown the aromatic foliage in summer. This sun-lover is an excellent selection for edging, clipping, or growing in pots.

Syringa vulgaris
LILAC
SHRUB; HARDY TO ZONE 3

Dense panicles of sweetly perfumed flowers in shades of white, pink, purple, and wine make this popular shrub a treat for the nose and the eye when in bloom. It likes either sun or shade, and flowers are good for cutting; split stems to prevent flowers from wilting too soon.

Habitat Gardens

Many gardeners strive to transform their backyards into small havens for visiting wildlife. The presence of a hummingbird, bluebird, or monarch butterfly is often considered a real compliment. Birdsong and brightly colored butterflies not only add beauty to the environment, but they also make the garden seem more like a natural refuge.

Feeders work wonderfully, of course, but habitat gardeners will do well to purposely grow the fruits, berries, and flowers that constitute the natural diet of the species they wish to attract. Water is also a must, whether the source is a natural brook, a small fountain, or simply a birdbath. It is important also to provide the animals with a secure environment by including plant and landscape elements for hiding and housing. This natural approach will achieve great results and will also benefit the animals, as their normal behavior patterns and diet will not be altered in any way by enjoying the resources of the natural setting re-created in the garden.

Right: *A generously planted area such as this provides the seeds, nectar, berries, and housing material that will draw a variety of wildlife to complement the flowers and fragrances of the garden.*
Above: Gaillardia pulchella.

Right: *A careless-looking mix of grasses and perennial wildflowers provides both nectar and larval hosts for several species of butterfly. Butterflies seem to especially enjoy feeding from the multitude of tiny florets found in the center of compound daisylike flowers; examples include these purple and white coneflowers* (Echinacea purpurea), *gray-headed coneflowers* (Ratibida pinnata), *and black-eyed susans* (Rudbeckia hirta) *blooming here.*

Opposite page: *A good way to attract butterflies is to include a variety of nectar plants in a border or bed. Plants such as cleome, zinnia, and euphorbia may prove useful. A local nursery will undoubtedly be able to suggest native flowers that are favored by the butterflies in your region; butterflies are most likely to come and sample the nectar of familiar flowers that are a natural part of their habitat.*

Left: *A successful butterfly gardener has managed to attract a number of beautiful swallowtail butterflies to this stand of purple coneflowers. Different butterfly species exhibit different meal preferences; monarchs seem to love feeding on liatris, while wild lupines in sandy Eastern areas sometimes provide nectar for the rare Karner blue butterfly.*

Right: *A large-scale, meadowlike space is not always needed in order to attract wildlife. This small garden contains nectar sources such as salvia for hummingbirds as well as gaillardia, butterfly weed, and rudbeckia for butterflies. Planting native flowers such as those featured here is good for the environment; the plants offer food sources for the birds and butterflies whose natural food supplies may be scarce in built-up areas.*

Right: *A single specimen of native* Lobelia cardinalis, *an excellent garden plant for either sun or shade, is all that was necessary to induce this swallowtail butterfly to stop for a sip. The wild cattails pictured in the background of this naturalistic setting could serve as food and nesting material for birds.*

Opposite page: *As shown here, growing wildflowers in a meadow-style garden to attract wildlife can be done in a surprisingly small space. The various species in this planting will appeal to hummingbirds as well as to butterflies. The inviting chair offers a lovely vantage point from which to observe the flowers and any small creatures that come to visit them.*

Right: *Large areas conceived, designed, and planted as natural habitats are in some ways a very modern idea, but the practice may have its origins in 18th-century English landscape designers and their ideas about improving on nature's own schemes. Ponds such as this one, whether natural or artificial, seem to develop their own ecosystems: Birds, butterflies, and even frogs come for the food provided by the flowers and insects that thrive near the water.*

Left: *This beautiful New Jersey garden combines three environments (woodland edge, garden border, and pond) into a site that is certain to attract wildlife of many kinds. Birds, butterflies, and small woodland mammals such as rabbits and chipmunks will find nectar, seeds, berries, water, and shelter here. The pond may also contain fish and amphibians and attract water birds, thus adding further to the wild population likely to enjoy this lovely spot.*

Techniques for attracting birds to the garden do not have to consist solely of natural ones. Houses, feeders, and birdbaths are traditional elements that are useful and also add a lovely decorative note without being too obtrusive. These charming birdhouses are carefully positioned near to sources of food—seed-bearing flowers (above) *and crabapples* (right).

Right: *Wildlife habitats include the woodland as well as meadows and ponds. Shaded yards, where grass and flowers are reluctant to grow, are often considered a gardening problem, but planting shade-loving wildflowers in such an area will create the appearance of a woodland glade and turn a problem into an asset. The pink-and-white combination of fringed bleeding heart (Dicentra eximia) and foamflower (Tiarella cordifolia) makes a lovely display above the rich green of their leaves.*

Left: *Cultivated varieties of native wildflowers often combine well with each other. Aquilegia canadensis 'Corbet' and Heuchera 'Montrose Ruby' are, respectively, pale-flowered and purple-leaved forms of a plant that occurs naturally with red-and-yellow blooms and medium-green leaves. Phlox stolonifera 'Pink Ridge' completes the picture for an area that is both lovely to look at and attractive to hummingbirds.*

 Above: *This beautiful stretch of wildflowers and ferns, which includes phlox, azalea, columbine, and trillium, is canopied by mature shade trees. Many small animals and birds will find this woodland setting as attractive as humans do and will eagerly make use of its ample food and nesting fodder. The winding paths allow for leisurely walks through the area without unduly disturbing the resident wildlife.*

Above: A cascade of frothy white bloom tumbles over the bank of a stream, repeating the movement of the rushing current. Beautiful natural wilderness scenes such as this can be copied most effectively in the home garden, but it is important to purchase wild plant species from reputable suppliers and not to dig them from the wild. In this way, woodland gardens may be created without destroying the beauty and integrity of the original.

Right: The elegance of simple, single blossoms shows especially well when they are planted en masse, as done here. White violets, blue woodland phlox, ferns, columbine, and hardy geranium make this small corner a thing of great beauty that captures the spirit of the wilderness within the confines of a yard.

Left: *Plants and wildlife have a reciprocal relationship; the botanicals are a source of nectar and seed, and in return, the plants' blossoms are pollinated by the creatures that use them for food. Here, a thriving colony of violets is joined by two other woodland natives, white foamflower* (Tiarella) *and the large-leaved mayapple* (Podophyllum peltatum), *in a dense border that is sure to entice a variety of the area's endemic woodland fauna.*

ACTAEA PACHYPODA
WHITE BANEBERRY; WHITE COHOSH
PERENNIAL; HARDY TO ZONE 3

This compact, clump-forming perennial prefers shady woodland conditions. Its springtime clusters of white flowers are followed in autumn by scarlet stalks bearing clusters of white berries, which are poisonous to humans but are a food source for some wildlife.

ALLIUM CERNUUM
NODDING ONION;
FLOWERING ONION
BULB; HARDY TO ZONE 4

Butterflies are especially fond of the small rose or white blossoms of this flowering onion, which are borne in loose, gracefully drooping umbels. This summer-blooming bulb prefers to enjoy full sun and requires good drainage.

AQUILEGIA CANADENSIS
WILD EASTERN COLUMBINE
PERENNIAL; HARDY TO ZONE 3

This familiar native wildflower is also a valuable garden plant. Its red-and-yellow flowers are smaller than those of its hybrid relations but have a charm all their own. A wonderful choice to attract hummingbirds, this elegant perennial likes a sunny spot and will often re-seed.

ASARUM CAUDATUM
WILD GINGER
PERENNIAL; HARDY TO ZONE 4

This species of wild ginger, native to western North America, makes a very attractive ground cover for shade with its heart-shaped, glossy green leaves. Small brown or reddish flowers with long tails on the petals appear in early summer but are hidden by the leaves.

ASCLEPIAS TUBEROSA
BUTTERFLY WEED
PERENNIAL; HARDY TO ZONE 3

As its common name indicates, this plant is a favorite food of butterflies, especially swallowtails and monarchs. A relative of milkweed, it produces bright orange flowers in summer and follows them with pointed seed pods. It likes full sun and is sensitive to root disturbance.

ASTER NOVAE-ANGLIAE
MICHAELMAS DAISY;
NEW ENGLAND ASTER
PERENNIAL; HARDY TO ZONE 3

This fall-blooming perennial produces loose corymbs of small, daisylike flowers atop tall stems in shades of pink, red, and lavender. Informal but attractive, it does best in moist soil and will mix well with other wildflowers and perennials.

ECHINACEA PALLIDA
PALE CONEFLOWER
PERENNIAL; HARDY TO ZONE 4

Mauve-pink flowers top 3–5′ stalks in summer and fall, making this a good candidate for planting by a fence or in the back of a wildflower border. Like its relative the purple coneflower (*E. purpurea*), it is visited by butterflies and bees and makes a good cut flower.

EUPATORIUM MACULATUM
JOE PYE WEED
PERENNIAL; HARDY TO ZONE 3

This very tall native prairie flower presents generous umbels of rose-purple flowers above whorls of narrow, pointed foliage. It will grow in either meadow or border with adequate sun and water. Bees love this flower and can sometimes be seen resting atop the blossoms on fall evenings.

GAILLARDIA PULCHELLA
BLANKET FLOWER
PERENNIAL; HARDY TO ZONE 4

When butterflies visit these red, orange, and yellow blooms, they add an extra dash of color to an already colorful plant. Though perennials, they are short-lived and are often grown as annuals. Full sun with good drainage is best.

GERANIUM MACULATUM
WILD GERANIUM
PERENNIAL; HARDY TO ZONE 3

This pretty American wildflower, with its dainty, pink to lilac-white flowers, makes a good candidate for the perennial border, wildflower garden, or meadow garden. It will grow in either sun or shade and the scalloped leaves turn to red or tan in autumn.

HIBISCUS MOSCHEUTOS
ROSE MALLOW
PERENNIAL; HARDY TO ZONE 4 WITH PROTECTION

This shrubby, compact perennial produces huge, round, satiny flowers in pink, red, rose, white, or bicolors from midsummer to frost. Hummingbirds especially like the darker red and rose-colored flowers. Full to part sun and moist soil are best.

ILEX SPECIES
SHRUB

This genus includes a variety of hardy to moderately hardy shrubs. Most bear berries in winter, which birds and other wildlife may eat. Winterberry (*Ilex verticillata*), American holly (*Ilex opaca*), and English holly (*Ilex aquifolium*) are three widely grown species.

LOBELIA CARDINALIS
CARDINAL FLOWER
PERENNIAL; HARDY TO ZONE 3

The cardinal flower's bright scarlet, tubular flowers are borne in midsummer over medium-green, lance-shaped leaves, making an especially pretty sight when they are visited by hummingbirds. This North American wildflower grows well in part sun to shade.

MERTENSIA VIRGINICA
VIRGINIA BLUEBELLS
PERENNIAL; HARDY TO ZONE 4

This elegant, blue-flowered wildflower blooms in spring, and the foliage dies down by midsummer, to re-emerge the following spring. Shade and a moist soil are best; it does well in a wild woodland area or in the shady border.

MONARDA FISTULOSA
WILD BERGAMOT
PERENNIAL; HARDY TO ZONE 3

This wild relative of hybrid bee balms makes a good candidate for the perennial border or for the wild garden. Lilac-purple flowers, which bees, butterflies, and hummingbirds love, bloom from midsummer to fall.

PACHYSANDRA PROCUMBENS
PACHYSANDRA; ALLEGHENY SPURGE
PERENNIAL; HARDY TO ZONE 4

This genus of creeping, shrubby perennials includes some of the best ground-cover plants for shady areas. Its spreading stems sprout clusters of pale pink flowers in the spring and are topped by whorls of blue-green, rounded leaves.

Phlox divaricata
WILD BLUE PHLOX; WOODLAND PHLOX
PERENNIAL; HARDY TO ZONE 4

The peak blooming season for this pretty American native species is early, in April and May. An excellent choice for shade, it requires little attention. The flowers are pale in color and shaped like blunted stars.

Phlox stolonifera
CREEPING PHLOX
PERENNIAL; HARDY TO ZONE 4

Small, cup-shaped flowers cover the leaves of this low-growing species with clusters of pink, lavender, blue, or white blossoms in early summer. This phlox loves shade, moisture, and a humus-enriched soil.

Podophyllum peltatum
MAYAPPLE
PERENNIAL; HARDY TO ZONE 4

Deeply lobed leaves emerge in spring folded in umbrella fashion. After they spread out, white flowers appear and are followed in autumn by rounded fruits. At 12–18″ tall, this American native does well in a woodland setting with moist soil, and it will naturalize.

Primula paryii
PRIMULA; PRIMROSE
PERENNIAL; HARDY TO ZONE 3

The bright red to purple color of the flowers and the blooming time in early summer make this an unusual primrose. Like others, though, it will thrive under open woodland conditions where summers are cool, and it makes a good addition to a wildflower collection.

Ratibida pinnata
PRAIRIE CONEFLOWER; MEXICAN HAT
PERENNIAL; HARDY TO ZONE 3

A raised central cone and narrow, drooping, yellow petals compose the blooms of this tall wildflower, which does very well in a meadow planting or in the border. It requires a sunny spot, will do well in most soils including clay, and is attractive to butterflies.

Sanguinaria canadensis
BLOODROOT
PERENNIAL; HARDY TO ZONE 3

Bloodroot, so named because of the red sap exuded when its underground stems are cut, is a pretty, elegant, and very hardy wildflower. White blossoms appear in spring before the large, scalloped leaves emerge. It does well in sun or shade.

Salvia azurea
AZURE SAGE
PERENNIAL; HARDY TO ZONE 4

This Midwestern native supplies a source of blue flowers in late summer, a rare color at that season. Good for naturalizing or in a border, this 3–4′ tall plant likes sun and good drainage, and it is a favorite of both hummingbirds and butterflies.

Silphium perfoliatum
CUP PLANT
PERENNIAL; HARDY TO ZONE 3

This large (to 10′ when mature) plant needs space, but wherever planted, in border or meadow, it is sure to attract wildlife. Small cups formed at the juncture between stem and leaf hold water and are visited by birds and butterflies wanting a drink. Goldfinches like the seeds.

SOLIDAGO RIGIDA
STIFF GOLDENROD
PERENNIAL; HARDY TO ZONE **3**

The tall thick stalks of this plant carry fluffy, golden-yellow summer flowers in umbels. A native of the North American prairie, it is hardy but not invasive. It is well suited to a variety of soil types but likes full sun.

STYLOPHORUM DIPHYLLUM
CELANDINE POPPY
PERENNIAL; HARDY TO ZONE **4**

Flowers like pretty golden cups appear on wiry, branching stems over the lobed, large leaves in springtime. A woodland native, this hardy poppy is suited to shady settings, where the flowers seem to glow.

TELLIMA GRANDIFLORA
FRINGECUPS
PERENNIAL; HARDY TO ZONE **4**

Lobed, heart-shaped leaves are topped by slender wands of fringed, cream to white, bell-shaped flowers in spring. As they age, the flowers turn pink or reddish. A good ground-cover plant for shade, fringecups grow well even in poor soils.

TIARELLA CORDIFOLIA
FOAMFLOWER
PERENNIAL; HARDY TO ZONE **3**

Profuse panicles of airy, white blooms rise above the veined, medium-green leaves in late spring and early summer. A wonderful plant for the shaded or woodland garden, it will spread and make an attractive ground cover. It will also tolerate some sun.

UVULARIA GRANDIFLORA
MERRYBELLS
PERENNIAL; HARDY TO ZONE **3**

Related to the more familiar Solomon's seals, merrybell needs similar moist and shaded conditions; it will do well in a woodland area. Dainty, long, bell-shaped flowers dangle gracefully from slender, arching stems in spring.

VIBURNUM DENTATUM
ARROWWOOD
SHRUB; HARDY TO ZONE **4**

This 10′ North American native shrub is an excellent choice for attracting wildlife; reddish flower clusters, which are visited by bees, butterflies, and hummingbirds, are followed by black berries that birds like to eat. The strong, straight branches were once used to make arrows, hence its common name.

VIOLA STRIATA
STRIPED VIOLET
PERENNIAL; HARDY TO ZONE **4**

Like most other viola species, this American native likes shade during the heat of the summer, but it will take more sun in spring. A place beneath deciduous shrubs is ideal; it also does well in the woodland garden. Dainty, cream-colored flowers appear above the foliage in April or May.

ZIZIA AUREA
GOLDEN ALEXANDERS
PERENNIAL; HARDY TO ZONE **3**

This attractive native plant carries its springtime umbels of golden yellow flowers over shiny, divided green leaves. It enjoys both moist shade and sun. It makes a good plant for the woodland garden or a nice addition to a collection of prairie wildflowers.

Rock Gardens

Rock gardening is a fascinating subgroup of the horticultural arts. Re-creating alpine landscapes in miniature with natural dwarf perennials and delicate but hardy succulents and bulbs offers endless challenges and rewards to the gardener. The dainty scale of the plants also allows for great versatility in design, as they can be adapted to just about any size the grower desires. One can also play with scale and make a small space look larger by a studied placement of rocks and the addition of dwarf shrubs.

While a traditional rock garden is planted directly in the ground, a smaller but equally handsome form may be designed to fit a large trough using the same sort of miniature alpines featured in regular rock gardening. Walls or rock outcroppings can also be cultivated as a sort of vertical garden by filling the spaces with soil and planting alpines and small perennials, which will make a lovely cascading show when in bloom.

Right: *Purple* Aubretia deltoidea *and bright golden* Alyssum saxatile *spread like brilliant cushions over gray, lichen-encrusted rocks. Stones that are not wanted in other areas can be brought together and interlaid with soil to create a stunning rocky landscape. Above:* Iris pumila *'Yellow.'*

Opposite page: *Trough gardens isolate and raise miniature plants to make them more readily visible; the trough also acts as a frame, displaying these tiny landscapes to best advantage. Succulents such as sedum and sempervivum are combined here with miniature evergreens, creating an attractive year-round planting. Covering the soil with gravel helps the plants show up well and discourages weeds; larger stones are often added as well, to further the illusion of scale.*

Right: *Tiny-flowered alpine perennials and collections of succulents are two classic choices for filling troughs. The innovative arrangement shown here delights the eye by grouping several containers together; the variation in size and shape calls attention to the different collection each holds. In the foreground is an assortment of species of stonecrop, or sedum, while to left and right, pink saponaria and blue campanula spill over their respective containers.*

Above: *In times past, many gardeners reclaimed old English stone troughs and sinks to use as planters. Thus, the classic material for a planting trough is rough-cut stone, making them sturdy but extremely difficult to move. Materials such as wood or fiberglass can also be attractive and far easier to relocate. This beautiful wooden trough holds a wonderfully varied collection of hens-and-chicks.*

Right: *Unmortared stone walls are especially amenable to planting, as the spaces between stones may be used to hold pockets of soil to create additional areas for plant growth. The lines of this warm-colored stone wall have been softened by surrounding it with garlands of Alyssum saxatile (also known as Aurinia saxatilis) and Phlox subulata, while gold and orange wallflowers make a showy background.*

Opposite page: *This retaining wall marks a boundary between two levels; mat-forming plants have been cleverly positioned at the top so that their cascades of tiny blooms spill down the wall's surface to be seen at eye level from the path below. Purple aubretia, yellow alyssum, and the perennial white-flowered candytuft Iberis sempervirens are topped by a splash of red tulips for a scene full of spring exuberance.*

Right: *This gardener has taken advantage of the loosely laid drystone wall to plant along the top, on the face, and at its feet; plants both trailing and of upright growth can therefore be accommodated. In this case, the planting includes evergreens and shrubs as well as the ground cover (here seen as a wall cover) ajuga, imperata, and Argemone mexicana.*

Right: *Stone walls and steps are natural rock-garden sites, since many plants grow on rocky outcroppings in their native habitats. The stones regulate temperature by keeping the direct sun off roots and by retaining warmth even after the sun goes down, which the foliage appreciates. The shady steps shown here are graced with a handsome combination of lady's mantle* (Alchemilla mollis), *hart's-tongue fern* (Asplenium scolopendrium), *and a hardy, single-flowered fuchsia hybrid.*

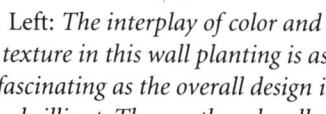

Left: *The interplay of color and texture in this wall planting is as fascinating as the overall design is brilliant. The weathered wall composed of flint and brick draws character from its covering of handsome-colored lichens and comes alive with the generous sprinkling of the golden-flowered stonecrop* Sedum acre, *which grows along the top of the wall as well as in vertical pockets. Tendrils of dark green ivy* (Hedera helix) *wind through at top left.*

Above: *Mortared walls often allow space for plants to take root at the top and base of the wall, and half-planters may be filled with trailing plants and hung at intervals to cover the surface. Apricot, red, and yellow shades of the sun-loving rock rose helianthemum spill over the top of this wall and exhibit their natural cascading growth habit.*

Above: A fine example of the widely appealing alpine and dwarf plant garden, this charming and diverse planting has each plant spaced and positioned so that it may be individually inspected. Alpine gardens, a rock garden subtype, contain collections of miniature plants from alpine regions, usually planted on a slope composed of rocky scree; they often contain plants that are rare or scarce and are true collector's items.

Left: *Whereas alpine gardens usually feature one or two examples of each plant and put emphasis on the extent of the collection, traditional rock gardens are composed with an eye for design. Multiples of the same species are often used for the beauty of the color effect this creates. Here, clouds of white alyssum are interspersed with the flowers of magenta-colored sea pink (Armeria maritima) and with succulents such as agave.*

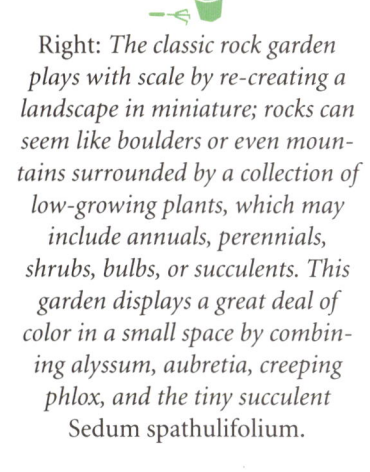

Right: *The classic rock garden plays with scale by re-creating a landscape in miniature; rocks can seem like boulders or even mountains surrounded by a collection of low-growing plants, which may include annuals, perennials, shrubs, bulbs, or succulents. This garden displays a great deal of color in a small space by combining alyssum, aubretia, creeping phlox, and the tiny succulent Sedum spathulifolium.*

Right: *Close access to the small botanicals used in rock gardening is important for best viewing; many can be easily obscured by larger plants or can be difficult to appreciate from a distance. Raising the plants in troughs, on walls, or against slopes is one option; another is creating paths or trails that allow access to materials located away from the garden's margins, as is done here with the large, flat stepping-stones.*

Left: *A meandering footpath composed of natural-looking, irregularly shaped paving stones beckons the garden visitor to walk under the trees to see, touch, and smell the fragrant creeping thyme that spreads across the base of this slope. Ferns and sea pinks mix attractively with the herbs. A separate set of paving stones leads up the hill for even closer appreciation of the plant life.*

Left: *Carpets of emerald-green moss, brightly flowering aubretia and alyssum, and silvery, succulent sedum are tucked into pockets at different levels, allowing for an ever-changing view all the way up these rough-hewn rock steps. Without planting, the dark gray rocky outcropping could easily look bleak; when decorated with a rock garden, it takes on a softer, prettier, and more welcoming character.*

Opposite page: *Intriguing effects can be achieved by combining two styles of garden in close conjunction. Here, a slope of rocky terraces supporting rock-garden plants ends with a water spout emptying into an ornamental pond. Water-loving* Iris laevigata *'Variegata' and the less-thirsty lady's mantle* Alchemilla mollis *can therefore be grown close to each other. The arrangement creates a lovely image as the vertical iris foliage reaches up toward the alchemilla leaves that spill over the rocky edge.*

Right: *Pools of water set off a rock garden that stretches along the banks of a small stream. The water will increase humidity and lower temperature by evaporation, tempering the site so that the rocks located in full sun do not become too hot for the plants. An eclectic mix of blooming, mat-forming perennials and evergreens in prostrate, conical, and globular shapes makes for a beautiful, dense alpine re-creation.*

Opposite page: *This naturally rocky yard has been skillfully altered to create an impressive expanse of greenery. The cliffs at rear hide behind a variety of shrubs and climbers. In the foreground, prostrate junipers and dwarf Japanese maples contribute shape and texture to a multilevel garden, while flowering tulips and azaleas add dashes of color. Young evergreens at right are protected with rocky collars to prevent them from washing away.*

Right: *Rather than removing large objects such as stones, logs, and stumps, clever gardeners can use them as focal points. The variegated gray tones of the two boulders at the side of this field are complemented by indigo* Baptisia australis *and contrasted by the warm orange of a hybrid honeysuckle. The upright form of the baptisia and the rounded, flowing lines of the honeysuckle are also set off by the flat, weathered shapes of the rocks.*

Above: *Great Plains native* Yucca glauca *creates a strong presence among these rocks. Backed by evergreen and deciduous trees as well as flowering shrubs, this spot has the look of a Western wilderness. The combination is effective and interesting; yucca thrives in the heat trap created by the outcrop, and its spiky, gray-green leaves and handsome upright flowers stand out from the rounded shapes of the dun-colored stones and the deeper green leaves of the trees.*

Right: *This isolated boulder above the thin soil of an outcropping has been called into service as a rock garden in miniature. Serving as both container and ornament, it takes on the significance of a piece of sculpture. Two species of the aptly named stonecrop, or sedum, appear here, throwing up spikes of flowers and clearly thriving in this dry, hot location.*

Right: *The site and situation of a rocky area determine what plants will do best there. The lean, dry soil and full sun of the previous single-stone garden suited succulents down to the ground; this area, thanks to the brook running through it, contains several microclimates. Sedum thrives here, too, but plants that require significantly higher moisture, such as ferns, are also accommodated.*

Opposite page: *Small deciduous specimen trees are allowed to show off the graceful shape of their branches against a flat expanse of smooth rock. The heavy ground cover provides bright, contrasting color with a sea of fuchsia foliage. The new leaves at the tips of the branches on the purple-leaved shrub in the background exactly match the ground cover for color.*

AQUILEGIA FLABELLATA
JAPANESE FAN COLUMBINE
PERENNIAL; HARDY TO ZONE 4

The dainty, nodding, bonnet-shaped flowers and the attractive blue-green foliage make these plants a welcome addition to any garden. Their small size (6–12″ tall) and compact habit of growth make them a good choice for a rock or trough garden.

ARABIS CAUCASICA 'SNOWCAP'
ARABIS; WHITE ROCK-CRESS
PERENNIAL; HARDY TO ZONE 4

This classic rock-garden plant produces attractive, spreading mats of evergreen foliage, with an abundance of small white flowers appearing in April. Arabis tolerates full sun and does well in a dry area or on a slope with good drainage.

ARMERIA MARITIMA
SEA PINK; THRIFT
PERENNIAL; HARDY TO ZONE 3

The small size (to about 6″ tall) and clumping habit of this perennial make it excellent for edging or for rock gardens. Round heads of pink or white flowers are carried over the narrow, grassy foliage. The effect is similar to that of chives, but prettier and more compact.

ASPLENIUM SCOLOPENDRIUM
HART'S-TONGUE FERN
FERN; HARDY TO ZONE 4 WITH PROTECTION

This fern has leathery, medium-green, undivided fronds, and the margins of some varieties are wavy, making them especially decorative. A good plant for the shady or waterside rock garden, it rarely grows over 1′ tall. It will also grow on walls.

AUBRETIA DELTOIDEA
AUBRETIA
PERENNIAL; HARDY TO ZONE 4

Along with arabis and aurinia, this is one of the three classic spring-blooming plants for rock gardens. The low, spreading leaves form a mat that is covered with a carpet of purple blooms in springtime. It makes a perfect choice for planting on a bank, wall, or slope.

AURINIA SAXATILIS
GOLDEN ALYSSUM; BASKET-OF-GOLD
PERENNIAL; HARDY TO ZONE 4

A profusion of small, brilliant yellow flowers makes this plant a cheerful sight in springtime, and its low, spreading habit makes it a good choice to combine with arabis and aubretia. The flowers of the variety 'Citrina' are a softer, more pastel shade of yellow.

CAMPANULA COCHLEARIFOLIA
BELLFLOWER; FAIRY'S THIMBLE
PERENNIAL; HARDY TO ZONE 5

Rosettes of small round leaves spread along runners and produce clusters of dainty pale blue or white bells on delicate, wiry stems in summer. This perennial is compact, pretty, and easily grown in a sunny spot. Its size makes it perfect for rock gardens and containers.

CERASTIUM TOMENTOSUM
SNOW-IN-SUMMER
PERENNIAL; HARDY TO ZONE 4

Tiny white flowers, held closely above the narrow gray foliage, bloom from late spring all through the summer on this excellent ground-cover plant. It enjoys a hot, dry situation in full sun and is excellent for covering a bank or growing on top of a wall to cascade down the front.

DELOSPERMA COOPERI
ICE PLANT
PERENNIAL; HARDY TO ZONE 6

Bright purple-magenta flowers of daisylike form appear over the succulent leaves of this sun-lover in summer. A good choice for banks, rock gardens, or beside a sunny walkway, this low-growing plant makes a cheerful splash of color for a dry, well-drained area.

DEUTZIA GRACILIS
DWARF DEUTZIA
SHRUB; HARDY TO ZONE 5

This dwarf form of a popular genus of shrubs makes a good addition to an area where space is at a premium. Arching branches bear double white flowers in spring and foliage that turns an attractive red in fall. Forms with rose-colored blooms are also available.

DIANTHUS DELTOIDES
MAIDEN PINK
PERENNIAL; HARDY TO ZONE 4

Single five-petaled flowers with serrated edges in shades of pink, mauve, red, or white make a bright show in summer above the tiny leaves. If cut back after flowering, it will rebloom in fall. It makes a nice ground cover in the rock garden and even in containers.

DRYAS OCTAPETALA
MOUNTAIN AVENS
PERENNIAL; HARDY TO ZONE 3

Creamy white flowers with sunny yellow centers bloom from summer to fall above tiny, leathery, bright green leaves, which remain green in winter. Attractive seed heads follow the flowers. Drought tolerant and sun loving, this plant looks nice in a trough garden.

ERYSIMUM SPECIES
WALLFLOWER
HARDINESS VARIES

This genus includes annuals, biennials, and perennials of varying heights and degrees of hardiness. All bear single or double spring-blooming flowers in shades including yellow, bronze, white, orange, and red, which are good for slopes, rock gardens, or for growing against a wall.

FESTUCA OVINA
BLUE FESCUE
PERENNIAL GRASS; HARDY TO ZONE 4

This compact, tuft-forming grass has narrow leaves in beautiful shades of silvery blue-green. As the plants grow no taller than 4″, it makes an excellent grass for edging or for small-scale plantings.

GENTIANA ACAULIS
TRUMPET GENTIAN; STEMLESS GENTIAN
PERENNIAL; HARDY TO ZONE 4

Trumpet-shaped flowers of an unusual hue (dark navy blue with darker, green-striped throats) sit on very short stems above spreading foliage. Blooming in the spring and often again in fall, it makes a wonderful choice for troughs or gardens.

GERANIUM DALMATICUM
DWARF PINK GERANIUM
PERENNIAL; HARDY TO ZONE 4

Pretty, shell-pink, five-petaled flowers bloom in summer over attractively divided, glossy, dark green leaves that turn red to orange in autumn. This plant makes a nice pastel-toned accent for rock gardens, and it will spread nicely. It likes a bit more shade than many rock garden plants.

GYPSOPHILA REPENS
BABY'S BREATH
PERENNIAL; HARDY TO ZONE **4**

HELIANTHEMUM SPECIES
ROCK ROSE
SHRUB; HARDY TO ZONE **6**

IBERIS SEMPERVIRENS
CANDYTUFT
PERENNIAL; HARDY TO ZONE **4**

IRIS PUMILA
DWARF BEARDED IRIS
PERENNIAL; HARDY TO ZONE **4**

A multitude of tiny pink, rose, or white flowers are borne in such profusion above the narrow, blue-green leaves that they create a misty effect when viewed from a distance. A prostrate habit makes this sun-lover a graceful accent for bank, wall, or rock garden.

Helianthemums should not be confused with the genus *Cistus,* also commonly called rock roses. An excellent grace note for a sunny bank, walk, or rock garden, these small shrubs bear tiny rose-shaped flowers in midsummer, after which they should be cut back.

Spring-blooming clusters of sweetly scented, pure white flowers on spreading plants make candytuft an excellent companion for small, spring-blooming bulbs in a rock garden. A trim after flowering helps to keep the plant healthy and full.

These winsome relatives of the familiar standard bearded iris have flowers that repeat their taller relatives' in miniature, but their blooming season is earlier. Dwarf bearded irises come in many colors, and their stature makes them excellent for the rock garden.

LEWISIA COTYLEDON
LEWISIA
PERENNIAL; HARDY TO ZONE **6**

LINUM PERENNE
BLUE FLAX
PERENNIAL; HARDY TO ZONE **3**

OPUNTIA HUMIFUSA
PRICKLY PEAR
CACTUS; HARDY TO ZONE **4**

PENSTEMON HIRSUTUS
HAIRY PENSTEMON
PERENNIAL; HARDY TO ZONE **4**

A good choice for growing in rock gardens, troughs, or pots, this native of the Pacific Northwest blooms in ice-cream colors of pink, peach, apricot, cream, and white. Water should not be allowed to remain for long in the foliage rosettes as this may damage the plants.

This perennial of delicate appearance has flowers of an unusually clear shade of blue; it combines well with pinks and yellows. Slender upright stems clothed in tiny leaves form a vase shape, making this a good accent when used with lower-growing plants.

This species of prickly pear is hardy only in warmer areas; however, where it may be grown outside, its unusual prostrate pattern of growth fits well in rock gardens. Yellow flowers appear in spring to summer.

This floriferous late-spring bloomer produces spikes of rose-pink to lavender flowers above narrow, soft-haired oval leaves. The plants will thrive in crevices and on open ground. The selection 'Pygmaeus' grows only 2–3' tall.

PHLOX SUBULATA
CREEPING PHLOX
PERENNIAL; HARDY TO ZONE 3

A mounding habit and tiny, needlelike leaves form the background to star-shaped flowers borne in great profusion on this low-growing phlox. Its spring blooming time and compact size make it good for a rock garden or wall.

POLYPODIUM VIRGINIANUM
AMERICAN WALL FERN
FERN; HARDY TO ZONE 3

This attractive evergreen fern makes an excellent choice for planting in wall crannies or in small spaces in partly shaded rock gardens. A compact creeping fern, it has divided and pointed narrow fronds of a medium green.

SAPONARIA X LEMPERGII 'MAX FREI'
HYBRID SAPONARIA
PERENNIAL; HARDY TO ZONE 5

This plant's long, branching stems have a trailing habit, making it a good candidate for planting along steps or hanging over a stone wall. Small flowers of clear pink are produced from the height of summer to fall.

SEDUM SPURIUM
GROUND-COVER SEDUM
PERENNIAL; HARDY TO ZONE 4

Handsome succulent leaves on creeping stems make this a good ground cover for a sunny slope; it also grows well in a trough or on top of a wall. Domed clusters of star-shaped flowers vary in color from red to pink to white, and bloom in summer.

SEMPERVIVUM TECTORUM
HENS-AND-CHICKS; HOUSELEEK
SUCCULENT; HARDY TO ZONE 4

These low-growing succulents quickly form colonies by producing smaller offsets around their bases. The rosettes can be green, bronze, ruby, and green with darker tips. A favorite for pots, sunny garden spots, and troughs, this species is easy to grow.

THYMUS SPECIES
THYME
PERENNIAL HERB; HARDINESS VARIES

This genus includes many shrubs and subshrub herbs of prostrate or upright habit whose small leaves and flowers and compact shape make them good candidates for inclusion in a rock-garden planting. Trailing species are especially appropriate. Some have fragrant foliage.

YUCCA FILAMENTOSA
YUCCA; ADAM'S NEEDLE
PERENNIAL; HARDY TO ZONE 4

Large spikes of cream-colored, bell-shaped flowers bloom in summer and complement the dark green foliage, which bears unusual tendrils. Good as a specimen or planted in a group where there is room, this stately 6' perennial lends an exotic appearance when in bloom.

ZAUSCHNERIA CALIFORNICA
CALIFORNIA FUCHSIA
PERENNIAL; HARDY TO ZONE 7

Bright scarlet, tubular flowers appear from late summer to fall on these woody perennials with slender, pointed, gray-green leaves. The bright color and height (to 1') of this plant make it a good choice for creating variety among low, spreading plants. It also does well in a container.

Shade Gardens

While sunshine and good drainage are usually two of the most obvious prerequisites for laying out a garden plot, gardeners can still achieve remarkable and breath-taking displays in a space that lacks either or both. It is possible to get a lovely display of flowers even from a small plot on the north side of a building, an exposure that often gets little if any direct sunlight. Even consistently damp ground need not foil the garden-maker.

The secret lies in choosing plants carefully: Roses and delphiniums may languish in too much shade, but many equally beautiful plants love to hide from the sun. Hostas, ferns, and mosses will thrive in the shade, while flowering plants such as hellebores and rhododendrons are all much happier when out of the direct sunlight. Additionally, lilies and many other plants like to grow with their roots shaded but their tops in sunlight, which allows for a variety of placements.

Left: *As moss-covered steps wind gently upward through a shadowy dell, fuchsia-pink rhododendrons in full bloom light up a dark, cool spot near the path with their brilliant color.* Above: Dicentra eximia.

Above: *Not all shaded areas receive the same intensity of light. Lightly shaded spots get about four to six hours per day, medium shade averages about two to four, and heavily shaded locations such as the one shown may get less than two. This grouping creates a beauty spot with little direct sunlight. Primula species add low-growing notes of color, while the delicate leaves of various Japanese maples arch over an ornamental pond.*

Right: *Ferns and hostas are some of the best and most reliable choices for shade gardens because they are hardy, lush, and vigorous. The elegant leaves of Hosta 'Francee' and Dryopteris marginalis are here complemented by the all-white flowers of bleeding heart, tiarella, and sanguinaria. The light-colored flowers stand out especially well in the deep shade of this garden.*

Right: *Light is brought to a dark corner in this English garden through the inspired use of foliage plants. A variegated shrub almost appears to bear branches laden with blossom, so brightly do its white-edged leaves shine against a dark brick wall. Several species of ferns unfurl gracefully, and the ground cover is composed of baby's-tears in shades of lemon and lime.*

Opposite page: Hesperis matronalis, *also known as sweet rocket or dame's violet, is a fragrant biennial that is easily grown from seed. The dense, leafy plants make for a natural-looking planting while providing colorful, pleasantly scented blooms. They will respond well in a moderately shady area where they get two to four hours of sun per day. A double form of sweet rocket was grown in the eighteenth and nineteenth centuries but has been lost to cultivation.*

Right: *Perennial geraniums are beginning to receive due recognition as amazingly versatile garden performers. With a long season of bloom and no strong preference for sun or shade, they can be planted nearly anywhere. The pale blooms of* Geranium sylvaticum *'Album' dominate the foreground in this shady nook; background plants include penstemon, iris, and* Rodgersia tabularis.

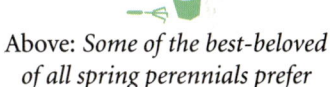

Above: *Some of the best-beloved of all spring perennials prefer shade over sun. This cheerful collection includes many species that have been cherished by gardeners for centuries, among them columbine, bleeding heart, Dog's-tooth violet, and the Labrador violet. A rare and beautiful hose-in-hose variety of primrose* (Primula vulgaris) *in pale yellow is a charming scene-stealer.*

Opposite page: *For many home-owners, having the screening and cooling benefit of shade trees on the property as well as the beauty of a blossom-filled flower garden represents the best of both worlds. By selecting plants that thrive in lightly shaded conditions, this gardener has created a harmonious picture in pink and white underneath a mature deciduous tree. Foxgloves, violas, impatiens, and some varieties of roses are among the species represented here.*

Right: *This beautifully crafted planting uses cultivated varieties of native species to create a woodland landscape that pays tribute to nature while clearly showing the influence of a human hand. The translucent pink blossoming prunus branches form natural garlands over cherry-pink rhododendron umbels, while white trillium adds a complementary accent. These species will all do well in a light-dappled corner such as this.*

Above: *Narcissus, tulips,* Anemone coronaria, *and* Iphion uniflorum *create a delicate floral carpet beneath a specimen tree. Spring bulbs such as these are good choices for planting beneath small trees and shrubs. They reap the benefits of direct sunlight in the early part of the year before the leaves of woody plants appear, but the ripening foliage is protected from the hotter sun of late spring and early summer as leaves mature.*

Right: *Hellebores, which include both the Lenten rose* (H. orientalis) *and the Christmas rose* (H. niger), *have long been a beloved addition to the spring garden. Despite the common names, the plants are no relation to roses, but they do make beautiful ground-covering colonies in shaded areas where conditions are right. While quite beautiful, they are also poisonous if ingested, so care should be taken when handling them.*

Right: *The right combination of species can create a varied and captivating ground-cover arrangement that would work well as a border or as a way to fill a shady spot against a house or wall. In this pleasing combination, variegated and plain-leaved ferns, hostas, and violets blend together into a richly patterned tapestry in shades of green and white.*

Left: *These naturalized plants, whose white and lilac-colored blooms seem to dance above the abundant foliage, completely carpet a shady border so that hardly a scrap of bare earth shows. Columbine, tiarella, and* Anemone nemorosa *bear flowers of snowy hue, while* Phlox x stolonifera *'Pink Ridge' adds a touch of color. Attractive, darkveined, purple leaves behind the phlox belong to* Heuchera x montrose *'Ruby.'*

Above: *The tremendous variation in leaf size and shape of these shrubs and perennials will hold the attention of anyone who might stroll down this shady path in the famous gardens of Hidcote Manor in England. The lush, green plants are growing so well that they spill over onto the stone-paved trail as they outline its curving shape. The epimedium on the left of the path is as lovely in foliage as it is in flower.*

Right: *The pleasingly pleated leaves and flowers of pure white* Trillium grandiflorum *rise out from the ground cover of pachysandra to bloom in early May. Trillium also goes by the enchanting common name of wake-robin. Many trilliums are still collected from the wild and then sold, so only purchase them if you can verify that they have been propagated by a nursery.*

Below: *A shaded rock garden offers the adventurous gardener space to experiment with rare or unusual plants. In this peaceful setting, the lesser-known relative of a more familiar garden plant contributes to a gently eye-pleasing picture.* Gaultheria shallon, *a cousin of the well-loved creeping winter-green* Gaultheria procumbens, *is set among* Polystichum muni-tum, *sword ferns, and bergenias. A scattering of pine needles emphasizes the woodland setting.*

Opposite page: *Candelabra primroses are excellent subjects for colorful springtime streamside gardens, as shown in the foreground. They mingle most agreeably with other plants that love both dampness and shade, such as hostas, irises, and rodgersia. Azaleas (backed by a wall of rhododendron flowers) burn with their own bright flame in the background, in tones matching those sported by the primroses.*

Right: *Unusually colored cultivars of familiar shade plants create a notably fresh and interesting look. Lobelia fulgens boasts leaves in deep plum tones to set off its scarlet flowers (which hummingbirds love), while the green-and-white striped leaves of Iris laevigata 'Variegata' are as neat and natty as a new straw boater. The lettucelike leaves in the foreground belong to primulas that have just gone out of bloom.*

Above: *The enormous, deeply lobed leaves of the perennial umbrella plant, Darmera peltata, naturally take center stage wherever they are planted. They make spectacular specimens for bog or water gardens but, being very large and invasive, are not suitable for small areas. Ferns and Siberian irises serve to lead the eye to a weathered gray bridge. The large gunnera in the background can be difficult to grow.*

Opposite page: *This innovative Japanese garden is a marvel of abstract gardening artistry. A great expanse of carefully cultivated moss is broken at irregular intervals by paving squares to create a not-quite-checkerboard pattern. Azaleas clipped in the shape of domes edge the expanse and are just beginning to show flushes of bloom. The scene as a whole has an unexpectedly entrapping yet soothing effect on the eye.*

Right: *A simple, pretty gazebo set amid mosses growing in the shade of these trees transforms a simple woodland scene into a haven of peace and tranquility. Strategically placed boulders serve as sculpture and invite contemplation, while shrubs enhance the decorative nature of the landscape design. Soft mosses underfoot muffle any outside noise and seem made to invite barefoot exploration.*

ANEMONE NEMOROSA
WOOD ANEMONE
PERENNIAL; HARDY TO ZONE **4**

This hardy perennial forms carpets of star-shaped, white or blue blooms in late spring above well-divided foliage. Preferring moist and shady woodland conditions, this anemone naturalizes well in a suitable environment to form large, attractive colonies.

ASARUM SHUTTLEWORTHII 'CALLAWAY'
SOUTHERN WILD GINGER
PERENNIAL; HARDY TO ZONE **4**

All hardy wild gingers make wonderful ground covers for shade. The primary attractions of this species are its heart-shaped, shiny leaves, marked with silver. The odd flowers, which are pitcher-shaped and dark brown, appear in early summer.

ASTRANTIA MAJOR
MASTERWORT
PERENNIAL; HARDY TO ZONE **4**

This clump-forming perennial has star-shaped flowers of greenish white, sometimes tinted pink or rose red. It will grow well in shade or sun and prefers a moist soil. The flowers are good in fresh or dried arrangements.

ATHYRIUM FELIX-FEMINA
LADY FERN
DECIDUOUS FERN; HARDY TO ZONE **3**

The light green, feathery, well-divided fronds of this fern have pointed tips and a graceful, arching habit. At 1–3′ tall, this is a compact fern, perfect for any garden spot with a shady aspect and moist soil.

BRUNNERA MACROPHYLLA
SIBERIAN BUGLOSS
PERENNIAL; HARDY TO ZONE **3**

Dainty sprays of dark blue flowers appear in spring, slightly preceding the dark green, ribbed leaves. An excellent plant for light shade, it may spread to become a deciduous ground cover. A variegated form is also available, which has a silver splash on the leaves.

CAREX SIDEROSTRICTA 'VARIEGATA'
VARIEGATED BROAD-LEAVED SEDGE
PERENNIAL; HARDY TO ZONE **4**

Broad green leaves generously striped in cream make this compact sedge a fine ornamental accent. Unlike many sedges, it tolerates shade and a moist soil, though it will also grow happily in sun. The handsome leaves will bring a touch of sunlight into a shady spot.

DARMERA PELTATA
UMBRELLA PLANT
PERENNIAL; HARDY TO ZONE **4**

This plant needs much room to spread out and show its lobed 2′ leaves, which are borne at the end of 3′ stems. Damp conditions suit it best; bog gardens with some shade are ideal. Pink to white flowers herald the appearance of the leaves in spring.

DICENTRA SPECTABILIS
BLEEDING HEART
PERENNIAL; HARDY TO ZONE **3**

The classic bleeding heart has pink-and-white, heart-shaped blooms carried on arching stalks above elegant fernlike foliage. A classic accompaniment to tulips and forget-me-nots, it puts on a lovely display in late spring; the foliage may disappear by midsummer, to appear again the following spring.

Epimedium grandiflorum
BARRENWORT; BISHOP'S HAT
PERENNIAL; HARDY TO ZONE 5

Shade or part sun will suit this low-growing perennial, which forms large clumps and makes a good ground cover. Compound leaves are light green, often flushed with pink or bronze in spring. The spurred flowers are white or rose and appear in spring.

Geranium maculatum
WILD GERANIUM
PERENNIAL; HARDY TO ZONE 5

This handsome perennial bears its heads of lilac-pink flowers primarily in spring. Its rounded, deeply lobed green leaves rise from a stout crown and turn attractive shades of tan, pink, and red in autumn. It will thrive in full sun to part shade and may be divided as it gets older.

Helleborus orientalis
HELLEBORE; LENTEN ROSE
PERENNIAL; HARDY TO ZONE 4

The downturned white, pink, or purple flowers of this clumping perennial appear in late winter or early spring, when bloom is scarce and flowers are especially welcome. They make excellent cut flowers, but all parts of the plants are poisonous. Dappled shade suits it best.

Impatiens walleriana
IMPATIENS
PERENNIAL; HARDY TO ZONE 8

This well-known tender perennial is a favorite summer bedding plant in almost all climates; where it is not hardy it is grown as an annual. Window boxes, pots, edging, and borders all suit these succulent-stemmed plants, as long as they are in shade and receive sufficient moisture.

Polystichum munitum
WESTERN SWORD FERN
FERN; HARDY TO ZONE 5

Handsome, well-divided fronds with an upright form, a lance-shaped outline, and a leathery texture characterize this attractive sword fern. Though an excellent choice for shade, it will also take some sun, as long as its roots receive sufficient moisture.

Primula japonica
CANDELABRA PRIMROSE
PERENNIAL; HARDY TO ZONE 4

Small flowers in shades of pink and red appear in early summer in outward-facing, circular layers around the 1–2′ stems. A lover of shade and moisture, this primrose makes a beautiful addition to a border or a streamside planting scheme.

Primula vulgaris
ENGLISH PRIMROSE
PERENNIAL; HARDY TO ZONE 3

The charming blossoms of this perennial are among the best-loved flowers of spring. Its compact size and ability to spread suit it to naturalizing or edging, and it prefers shade and moist soil. *P. v. sibthorpii* offers flowers in pink, red, and purple.

Pulmonaria saccharata
LUNGWORT; BETHLEHEM SAGE
PERENNIAL; HARDY TO ZONE 4

Small trumpet-shaped flowers open pink in spring and turn to blue as they age. The pointed, oval leaves are liberally splashed with silver and remain all summer or beyond if the weather is mild. This plant spreads and grows well in deep or dappled shade even with dry soil.

Water Gardens

Using water in gardens is part of an ancient tradition originating in India and the Middle East, where fountains and pools provided a soothing antidote to the stifling midday heat. Gardeners for the great houses of the aristocracy in England and France later adapted these ideas for use in more northerly climes, realizing that the presence of water can be a beautiful and restful addition to a garden in any climate.

Despite its grand beginnings, water gardening can be fitted to many different places and spaces. An in-ground pool or a small watertight tub on a patio can hold an assortment of aquatic plants, such as arrowheads, papyrus, and brightly blooming water lilies. A natural stream or pond affords many opportunities for planting everything from native cattails to exotic Japanese irises. Fountains, with their refreshing, melodious splashing sound, and birdbaths, with their accompanying wildlife, come in a wide variety of sizes and can fit even the smallest backyard.

Right: *In this whimsical fountain, a terra-cotta sun plaque inside a moon-shaped archway provides a centerpiece to a boisterous arrangement of roses and irises, including the yellow pond iris (Iris pseudacorus). Above: Nelumbo nucifera 'Queen.'*

Above: *This classically inspired Neptune fountain achieves grand formality on a small scale. While aquatic plants are growing in pots placed in the water, dwarf evergreens, regal lilies, and others that prefer drier conditions have been planted in pots positioned on stone or gravel. This clever method allows the grouping of plant species that favor a number of different growing conditions.*

Right: *Nature and artistry combine in this charming fountain, where a dragonfly sculpture encircles a small vertical waterspout. Whether on a large scale or small, formal or informal, the addition of water to a garden always creates a peaceful focal point.*

Above: *Even the smallest garden has space for a water feature; a glazed stoneware vessel makes a lovely water basin. The dark, neutral color of the pottery gives greater depth to the bright colors of the surrounding planting, which includes violet-flowered sweet garlic (Tulbaghia fragrans) in the left foreground and brilliant-leaved New Zealand flax (Phormium tenax 'Maori Sunrise') behind.*

Left: *This lovely basin with a central jet has the water set like a sapphire, flush with the surrounding emerald-green turf. This arrangement allows for an element of surprise, as the pool does not call attention to itself until the viewer is close by. A ring of hedges repeating the basin's round shape and a few pots of unobtrusive blooms are all the ornament this jewel of a pond needs.*

Right: *Raising a pool or fountain above the ground gives it added emphasis, allowing fountains to rise to greater heights and bringing the water closer to the viewer's level. This brick container with pool and fountain features a dark-colored liner, which makes the water appear deeper and cooler, and is surrounded by both in-ground plantings and plants in pots. The latter can be rearranged at any time to give a different frame to the pool.*

Left: *Another favorable aspect of above-ground water features is that small ones may be placed where in-ground pools are not appropriate, such as on a sturdy deck or patio. This clay-colored plastic container holds an entire miniature pond, planted with water lettuce and hybrid water lilies, including red Nymphaea 'James Brydon' and white 'Marliac albida.' Water lilies such as these are not always winter-hardy when grown in containers.*

Left: *A medium-size raised pool and fountain make a dramatic showpiece of a paved courtyard. The aquatic theme is carried through with a fish sculpture; boulders placed in the water look attractive and cleverly hide the fountain hardware and sculpture support. A few water plants are featured, but most of the planting is in movable pots.*

Right: *A circular, well-like pool in the ground near the house does double duty as a container for some plants and as a setting for others. Tropicals and hardy plants combine for a lush feel; lotus, canna, and several species of water lily fill the pool, which is completely surrounded by the gardenscape featuring irises and miniature daylilies.*

Right: *A small pond with water lilies set next to a grassy walk creates a storybook scene. The use of irregular stones gives the pond a natural look, which suits the rustic character of the garden. The stones further serve to disguise the pond liner. Nearly every artificial pond will need a vinyl or rubber liner to prevent water drainage.*

Left: *Combining two classic garden techniques can create some lovely effects in new and refreshing ways. Here, an in-ground pond is incorporated into a geometric knot-garden planting. One would expect the central round area to contain flowers, herbs, or a sundial; what a wonderful surprise to realize that it holds a pool in which water lilies are growing.*

Right: *Where space allows, including a larger pond or pool in the home landscape makes a great impact. A medium-size pond like this is an attractive adjunct to the patio and gives a much cooler feel than having the entire area paved or planted with lawn grass. The surrounding trees and perennial beds offer beauty and seclusion.*

Below: *The unbridled growth habits of aquatic plants adapt surprisingly well to the structured groupings in this long reflecting pond; one end is nearly the mirror image of the other. This arrangement also uses sweet flag and papyrus to achieve a very different but equally handsome effect. The large and beautiful white, pink, or fuchsia blooms of tropical water lilies are allowed to wander freely about the water's surface.*

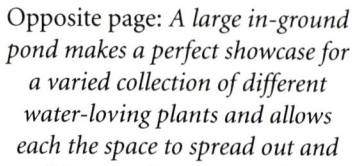

Opposite page: *A large in-ground pond makes a perfect showcase for a varied collection of different water-loving plants and allows each the space to spread out and achieve specimen proportions. This grouping includes papyrus, striped sweet flag (Acorus calamus 'Variegatus'), variegated iris, cattail, canna, and white-flowered water lily. Liriope makes an appearance in the bed in the foreground.*

Right: *Those fortunate enough to have a natural stream or creek running through their property have a strong point of interest that can be enhanced by landscaping along its margins. Here, flowering azaleas are planted side-by-side on the far bank to emphasize the stream's path. The small hemlock on the right accents the waterway nicely; its weeping branches echo the flowing movement of the water.*

Right: *Bright scarlet maple leaves, as beautiful as fallen blossoms, thickly cover bridge, stream, banks, and all in this lovely Pennsylvania garden. A bridge, no matter how small, always makes a pleasant addition to a brookside garden. It offers easy crossing and also allows for the observation of both garden and water from a new vantage point.*

Opposite page: *A waterwheel will add the interest of motion and the melodious, soothing sound of falling water to a garden scheme. This ornamental waterwheel feeds a winding, rock-lined stream, set in a perfect stretch of turf planted with flourishing hostas, ferns, and brightly blooming rhododendrons. Even a small stream will add beauty to the landscape and will also benefit plants by providing increased moisture at their roots.*

Opposite page: *Stone statuary of mythical figures and fountains spilling water into plant-lined ponds are among the oldest and most beautiful of gardening traditions. The setting pictured demonstrates these grand principles of design on a relatively small scale. Gardeners who incorporate similar inspirations and ideas into their home plantings can thus feel connected with the centuries of gardens and garden lovers who have gone before.*

Left: *When its use is well planned, water can achieve an enormous effect in a relatively small space. This pond uses the rugged beauty of slate boulders to create a dream of an alpine landscape. A small waterfall spills between the dark gray rocks, while the boulders themselves play host to a plethora of plants that are small in scale but bold in color.*

Left: *This small pond, extremely well blended into its landscape, is so thickly surrounded by foliage that its margins are blurred, giving the pond a natural appearance. Tall grasses at the verge of the pond repeat the vertical lines of the cattails planted in the water; fluffy astilbes in bloom further disguise the stone-ringed edge and complement the color of the water lilies in blossom. A trellised wooden pergola creates a further area of interest at the far end.*

Right: *This spacious stream-fed pond has been attractively edged with stones of different sizes, with the intent of calling attention to its outlines rather than hiding them. Various shrubs of different sizes and heights repeat the undulating rhythm of the pond's stony border. These are backed by rows of ever-taller shrubs and trees, while a wealth of perennials adds color and texture to the foreground and background.*

Opposite page: *Black, still water perfectly reflects the shapes of tall, slender tree trunks in this serene grouping of woodland plants, while spring-flowering hybrid azaleas in every imaginable shade of pink drop their delicate paper-like petals onto the pond's surface. Water always adds another dimension to a garden, though the manner in which it is used may vary greatly. Here, the water's reflection of the garden rivals the garden itself for capturing the observer's interest.*

Right: *This large pond is edged by herbaceous borders that appear to flow down the gentle surrounding slope to meet the water. The slope allows for good drainage, so that nonaquatic perennials such as the astilbe and sedum 'Autumn Joy' shown here may be planted without fear that their roots will become waterlogged, while water-lovers such as yellow canna, lotus, and water lily enjoy the environs of the pond itself.*

ACORUS GRAMINEUS
SWEET FLAG
PERENNIAL; HARDY TO ZONE 3

The grassy leaves of this water-loving perennial form an excellent vertical accent for a water garden. An especially attractive form, 'Variegatus,' has dark green leaves marked with cream. Its popular relative, *A. calamus,* is taller and less bushy.

COLOCASIA ANTIQUORUM
EGYPTIAN TARO; ELEPHANT'S EAR
PERENNIAL; HARDY TO ZONE 9

This large-leaved plant prefers part sun to part shade. It will do well in a waterside area or in a large tub with moist soil, but its 4′ stalks and 2′ leaves require lots of room. The 'Illustris' variety offers striking purple stalks and blotchy leaves.

CRINUM AMERICANUM
CRINUM
BULB; HARDY TO ZONE 9

Where it is not hardy, this amaryllis relative makes a good candidate for bedding out or container gardening and wintering indoors. A sunny spot with moist but well-drained soil suits this pretty summer-bloomer, but it will also grow submerged in a water garden.

CYPERUS ALTERNIFOLIUS
UMBRELLA PLANT
PERENNIAL; HARDY TO ZONE 9

In colder areas, this attractive sedge can be potted and placed outdoors directly in a garden pool when weather permits and taken indoors during the cold season. Narrow green bracts fan out in a palmlike circular pattern and sprout clusters of tiny green flowers in summer.

CYPERUS HASPAN
DWARF PAPYRUS
PERENNIAL; HARDY TO ZONE 9

The genus *Cyperus* comprises a group of handsome, water-loving sedges, many of which are wonderful additions to aquatic garden features. The dwarf papyrus produces green, moplike heads on sturdy stalks that reach 1–2′ above the water.

IRIS LAEVIGATUS
BEARDLESS JAPANESE IRIS;
JAPANESE WATER IRIS
PERENNIAL; HARDY TO ZONE 5

Sun or partial shade will suit these beautiful medium-size irises, whose intricate blue, purple, or white flowers are borne several to a stem in early summer. They will grow happily when planted either in shallow water or in a border with moist soil.

MARSILEA QUADRIFOLIA
WATER CLOVER
PERENNIAL; HARDY TO ZONE 5

This aquatic fern has compound, cloverlike leaves that sprout from long runners. A prolific spreader, it requires little effort to cultivate but must be cut back to keep it from overgrowing other species in the water garden.

NELUMBO NUCIFERA
SACRED LOTUS
PERENNIAL; HARDY TO ZONE 6

The large, floating, blue-green leaves of this aquatic plant are handsome on their own, but when topped by huge, pink, star-shaped blooms in summer, the plant takes on a truly spectacular appearance. The roots should be planted directly in the water.

NYMPHAEA ODORATA
FRAGRANT WATER LILY
PERENNIAL; HARDY TO ZONE 3

The lovely, waxen flowers of this hardy water lily are also fragrant. It may be planted directly in the mud or in a pot at the bottom of a pond and left to winter over. Either way, it prefers sun and still water.

NYMPHOIDES PELTATA
WATER-FRINGE;
YELLOW FLOATING-HEART
PERENNIAL; HARDY TO ZONE 7

Small fringed flowers of a cheerful yellow hue appear in summer above heart-shaped leaves. This deep-water plant is grown primarily for its attractive flowers, though the foliage is handsome as well. A sunny spot in open water suits it best.

ORONTIUM AQUATICUM
GOLDEN CLUB
PERENNIAL; HARDY TO ZONE 6

Yellow-and-white flower spikes of unusual appearance emerge with the floating oval leaves in spring and give this aquatic plant its common name. Golden club may be grown in shallow areas, and it lends an exotic touch to warm-climate water gardens.

PISTIA STRATIOTES
WATER LETTUCE
PERENNIAL; HARDY TO ZONE 8

Rich green floating leaves with attractively fluted edges will carpet a portion of the water's surface without taking over the entire expanse. Water lettuce is evergreen under tropical growing conditions and deciduous in the cooler portions of its range.

PONTEDERIA CORDATA
PICKEREL WEED
PERENNIAL; HARDY TO ZONE 3

Thick spikes of small periwinkle-blue flowers appear in summer among shiny, dark green leaves. An excellent selection for planting in the sun near the margin of a pond, it combines well with other aquatic plants and adds a welcome dash of beautiful color.

SAGITTARIA LATIFOLIA
ARROWHEAD
PERENNIAL; HARDY TO ZONE 3

The distinctive pointed leaves of this hardy and adaptable species give the plant its common name. Arrowhead loves a sunny spot in shallow water. Sprays of pretty, white, trefoil-shaped flowers on slender stems bloom in summer. The tuberous roots of this species are edible.

THALIA DEALBATA
WATER CANNA
PERENNIAL; HARDY TO ZONE 9

Stalks of tubular, reddish-purple flowers arise from large, broad, leathery leaves in summer; decorative seed heads follow. Both leaves and flowers are covered with a white powder. Unlike some tender tropical aquatics, this species will tolerate cool water.

TYPHA LATIFOLIA
CATTAIL
PERENNIAL; HARDY TO ZONE 3

The slender, graceful leaves and cylindrical brown seed heads of the common cattail are well known throughout North America. When planted in shallow water at the side of a pond, cattails will naturalize freely. Spikes of tan-colored flowers appear in late summer, followed by the velvety cattails.

Garden Suppliers

Ambergate Gardens
8015 Krey Ave.
Waconia, MN 55387
612-443-2248 phone/fax
martagon lilies, perennials, native plants and ornamental grasses, hostas

Blue Stone Perennials
7211 Middle Ridge Rd.
Madison, OH 44057
216-428-7535, 800-852-5243, Fax 428-7198
hardy perennials

Caprice Farm Nursery
15425 SW Pleasant Hill Rd.
Sherwood, OR 97140
503-625-7241, Fax 625-5588
hostas, Japanese and Siberian irises, daylilies, peonies

Carroll Gardens
P.O. Box 310
444 E. Main St.
Westminster, MD 21158
410-848-5422, 800-638-6334
perennials, herbs, roses, vines, conifers, trees and shrubs, spring and summer bulbs

The Daffodil Mart
7463 Heath Trail
Gloucester, VA 23061
804-693-3966, Fax 693-9436
spring and summer bulbs

Fancy Fronds
1911 4th Ave. West
Seattle, WA 98119
206-284-5332
hardy ferns

Fox Hill Farm
440 W. Michigan Ave.
Parma, MI 49269-0009
517-531-3179
herbs, scented geraniums, bee and dye plants

Greenlee Nursery
301 E. Franklin Ave.
Pomona, CA 91766
909-629-9045, Fax 620-6482
ornamental grasses

Klehm Nursery
4210 N. Duncan Rd.
Champaign, IL 61821
217-359-2888, 800-553-3715, Fax 373-8403
hostas, daylilies, irises, peonies, ferns, ornamental grasses, perennials

Kurt Bluemel, Inc.
2740 Green Lane
Baldwin, MD 21013
410-557-7229, Fax 557-9785
ornamental grasses, sedges and rushes, perennials, bamboos, ferns, aquatic plants

Lilypons Water Gardens
P.O. Box 10
6800 Lilypons Rd.
Buckeystown, MD 21717-0010
301-874-5133, 800-723-7667, Fax 874-2959
water lilies, lotus, bog plants

Milaeger's Garden
4838 Douglas Ave.
Racine, WI 53402-2498
414-639-2371, Fax 639-1855
seeds and plants of all kind

Sandy Mush Herb Nursery
Route 2, 316 Surrett Cove Rd.
Leicester, NC 28748
704-683-2014
herbs

Niche Gardens
1111 Dawson Rd.
Chapel Hill, NC 27516
919-967-0078
southeastern wildflowers and native plants, perennials, ornamental grasses, herbs

Plants of the Southwest
Route 6, Box 11A, Agua Fria
Santa Fe, NM 87501
505-471-2212, 438-8888
native trees and shrubs, wildflowers, grasses, cacti and succulents

Prairie Nursery
P.O. Box 306
Westfield, WI 53964
608-296-3679, Fax 296-2741
prairie plants and seed, grasses, herbs

John Scheeper, Inc.
P.O. Box 700
Bantam, CT 06750
203-567-0838, Fax 567-5323
bulbs

Van Ness Water Gardens
2460 N. Euclid Ave.
Upland, CA 91784
909-982-2425, Fax 949-7217
water garden plants and supplies

Andre Viette Farm & Nursery
Route 1, Box 16
State Route 608
Fishersville, VA 22939
703-942-2118, 942-2315, Fax 943-0782
garden perennials

Wayside Gardens
P.O. Box 1
Hodges, SC 29695-0001
800-845-1124
ornamental trees and shrubs, perennials, roses

We-Du Nurseries
Route 5, Box 724
Marion, NC 28752-9338
704-738-8300
rock garden and woodland plants

White Flower Farm
P.O. Box 50
Litchfield, CT 06759-0050
203-496-9600, Fax 496-1418
spring and summer flowering bulbs

Woodlanders, Inc.
1128 Colleton Ave.
Aiken, SC 29801
803-648-7522
southeastern native trees, vines, shrubs, ferns, ground covers, perennials

Index of Plants